CW01496447

FACE THE MUSIC

CHURCH & CHAPEL BANDS IN CORNWALL

Harry Woodhouse

CORNISH HILLSIDE PUBLICATIONS
ST. AUSTELL CORNWALL

FACE THE MUSIC

First published 1997 by
Cornish Hillside Publications
St Austell, Cornwall PL25 4DW.

ISBN 1900147 07 6 paperback
ISBN 1900147 08 4 hardback

Designed and set by Raymond Lancefield,
The Design Field, Truro, Cornwall.
Typeset in Utopia 9/10.5pt

Printed by R. Booth (Bookbinders) Ltd
Penryn, Cornwall.

CONTENTS

Harry Woodhouse with his serpent.

ABOUT THE AUTHOR

Harry Woodhouse was born in St. Austell in 1930 and went from St. Austell Grammar School to Queens' College Cambridge where he obtained his M.A. in Natural Sciences. He spent most of his working life as a manager for English China Clays, and his last job was to set up their Pacific office in Singapore. He lived there with his Cornish wife until he retired back to Cornwall.

An enthusiastic musical amateur, he has played the clarinet with the Cornwall Symphony Orchestra and other Cornish orchestras for over twenty years, and with a group of friends, he gives lecture-recitals for charity about the "Old Church Gallery Minstrels". He is a member of the West Gallery Music Association and the Galpin Society, and studies old musical instruments, making copies of them in his workshop. He plays many instruments including the serpent and the ophicleide and has made several TV appearances, including a short sequence in the "Poldark" series. He is a Bard of the Cornish Gorsedd.

Harry, his wife, and friends have had tremendous fun collecting the information for this book. They hope you have as much fun reading it.

ACKNOWLEDGEMENTS

Page No.

4 (bottom). Photo by courtesy of the Western Gazette, Yeovil.

7, 82 (bottom), 94. Reproduced from "The Music of the English Parish Church", by Nicholas Temperley, by kind permission of the author and Cambridge University Press.

9, 48 (top), 52. From "The Old Church Gallery Minstrels", by Canon K.H. MacDermott, SPCK, 1948.

10. From "Church and Chamber Barrel Organs", Langwill and Boston, Langwill, 1970.

12. Photo by Alan Tregaskes of St. Austell.

18 (top). Author's photo reproduced by courtesy of the Isles of Scilly Museum Association.

22, 68 (top). Author's photos reproduced by courtesy of the Cornwall Record Office.

31 (top). Author's photo reproduced by courtesy of the Royal Cornwall Museum, Truro, and the owners of the violin.

31 (bottom). Photo by Mr W.F.T. Davies of Tregear.

36, 59. From "Sussex Church Music in the Past" by Canon MacDermott, 1923.

38, 40. Photos by the Horniman Museum, London.

46. Reproduced from the front cover of "Punch" by courtesy of the publishers.

47. Photo by the Camborne-Redruth Packet.

48 (bottom). Reproduced by courtesy of the Royal Cornwall Museum, Truro.

49. Photo by Mrs Clarke of West Sussex.

50. Reproduced by courtesy of the Penlee House Art Gallery & Museum, Penzance.

51. Photo by Roger Dovey of St. Austell.

68 (bottom). Author's photo reproduced by courtesy of the Cornish Music Guild.

71. Photo by Mrs Wyatt of Truro.

74. Reproduced from "The Oxford Companion to Music", 1944, edited by Percy A. Scholes, by permission of Oxford University Press.

78 (bottom), 101. From "The Story of Cornwall" by A.K. Hamilton Jenkin, Thomas Nelson, 1934.

80 (bottom), 103, 104. Photo by John Black of Liskeard.

88. From "Kenwyn Church, Truro" by Arthur Gill, 1935.

102. Photo kindly provided by Mr Leslie Jenkin of Burnham-on-Sea.

80 (top). Copy supplied by Mrs Pat Phillipps of Mount.

Every effort has been made to trace holders of copyright. The author and publisher apologise if an acknowledgement has been inadvertently omitted.

PRE-FACE THE MUSIC.

Even professional authors often start their books with an apology, and this amateur author feels the need to do the same.

There are hundreds of books written about church music – perhaps special mention should be made of "The Music of the English Parish Church" by Professor Nicholas Temperley. No amateur author can hope to match such scholarly work.

This book therefore has a more limited objective – to get people interested in the church gallery minstrels, and to give them a quiet chuckle on the way. Little has been published on this rather specialised but fascinating topic.

The "classic" on this subject is Canon MacDermott's book "The Old Church Gallery Minstrels", SPCK, 1948. This delightful book has been out of print for some time, and copies are very difficult to find. His researches were concentrated on Sussex, rather giving the impression that the minstrels were more common there.

Here we have a strong bias towards Cornwall, which will perhaps redress the balance.

In a book of this kind, it was felt that putting reference numbers and acknowledgements throughout the text would be distracting to the general reader. All the significant references used are in the bibliography at the end, but the author begs forgiveness if a source has not been adequately acknowledged.

I would like to express my grateful thanks to the authors of the references used; to my wife and friends John and Caroline Black for helping with the research; to Dr Richard McGrady for his wise counsel; to Dr Philip Payton for permission to use material published in "Cornish Studies"; to Exeter University for a Caroline Kemp Research Scholarship which financed some of the work; to the librarians and staff of the Royal Institution of Cornwall, the Institute of Cornish Studies, and the County Record Office, Truro; to Rollo Woods and John Probert, and finally to my long-suffering publisher, Charles Thurlow, who has willingly learned about serpents and ophicleides to advise me how best to produce this book.

Porthpean 1996.

CHAPTER ONE

BACKGROUND

"Put the Kalandar back a couple of hundred years and come with me to some village church almost anywhere in England in, say, the year 1740 – or in any year between A.D. 1660 and 1860 for that matter. It is a Sunday, and the rustic community is slowly gathering for the morning service. Take your seat in that comfortless pew with the hard bench and the unyielding upright back. No, there are no cushions or hassocks, and the floor is of stone, tiles or uneven boards; there is no stove or heating gear, the building is cold and damp. The service will be long, the sermon, if there is one, longer still, and the spoken word will perhaps be as chilly and lifeless as the church. But there will be warmth and life in the gallery behind you, plenty of both, too much sometimes! You will hear a band of keen rural musicians, burning, and sometimes nearly bursting, with whole-hearted zeal for one of their chief delights in life. They are the Old Church Gallery Minstrels, the "musickers" or "musicianers", as their neighbours call them.

They are not robed in cassocks or surplices; probably clean smock-frocks are doing duty for the one and brown fustian, knee-breeches and buskins for the other. Simple and homely, rough-shod and heavy-handed, but zealous beyond words, very proud of their performance, though often noisy and unwittingly irreverent in doing it.

When they begin to play you will do as the other members of the con-gregation do – turn round to the west with your face to the gallery and your back to the altar, and literally "face the music" till it is finished".

Thus starts the introduction to the splendid book published in 1948 by Canon MacDermott, – "The Old Church Gallery Minstrels".

We are all so used to hearing the organ in our local churches and chapels, that it comes as something of a shock to realise that one hundred and fifty years ago many of them had no organ, and the singing was accompanied by a band of local musicians.

The organ has a long and distinguished history; indeed it was used by the ancient Romans. The oldest organ which is still playable is probably a charming little instrument in Sion, in Switzerland. In Britain, there was a monster organ in Winchester cathedral in the tenth century, which had four hundred pipes and required seventy strong men to work the bellows.It was described in a tenth century poem: "Like thunder the iron tones batter the ear .... The music is heard throughout the town, and the flying fame thereof is gone out over the whole country." No noise abatement societies in those days!

Over the centuries the organ matured into a more manageable instrument, and by the seventeenth century most cathedrals and large parish churches had them. The oldest organ recorded in Cornwall was at St. Ives, and was built in the fifteenth century at a cost of £30. Even in large parish churches the organs would have been smaller than the ones we see today, with restricted tonal resources and power. Small country churches simply could not afford an organ, and the singing was unaccompanied, as indeed it is today in the Greek Orthodox church.

THE COMMONWEALTH

Those churches which did have organs had a nasty surprise from Oliver Cromwell in 1644. His order in council demanded "The speedy Demolishing of all Organs, Images and all manner of Superstitious Monuments in Cathedrall, Parish Churches and Chappells, throughout the Kingdom of England and Dominion of Wales: the better to accomplish the blessed Reformation so happily begun, and to remove all offences and things illegal in the Worship of God."

Some organs in places of learning were spared – for example the famous Dallam organ in King's College Chapel, Cambridge. Some were "acquired" by the local gentry and re-installed in their houses.

A great many, however, were destroyed by the Commonwealth armies in a frenzy of Puritanical zeal. The St. Ives instrument thus succumbed in 1648, and John Matthews describes in his book "A History of St. Ives, Lelant, Towednack and Zennor" how for many years afterwards the pipes were to be seen around the town doing duty as drainpipes.It was not that the Puritans disliked music, or even that they disliked organs. Indeed Oliver Cromwell himself loved music: he had a church organ dismantled and re-erected in his home, and in 1657 he hired 48 violins and 50 trumpets for the wedding of one of his daughters.

To be fair to Cromwell, it should be said that the objections to organs in church had started in the reign of Henry VIII. Although Henry had severed the church connection with Rome, English services continued on the Roman model. Influence from the Protestants on the continent led to reaction against the pomposity of our church services, with little or no participation by the congregation. Organs were seen as part of this problem. In 1536 the Lower House of Convocation included organ-playing amongst the "84 Faults and Abuses of Religion". Services in the English language started in 1549, in the reign of Edward VI, and in 1563, in the reign of Elizabeth I, a resolution calling for the removal of all organs from places of worship was lost by a single vote.

As a result of all this, there was no organ music in our churches for the duration of the Commonwealth. On the restoration of the monarchy in 1660, organs were rapidly built in cathedrals and large churches, in many cases using the remains of instruments which had partially escaped destruction. Unfortunately, resources were not available to build organs for the small parish churches. There was not enough money, nor were there enough organ-builders. So from some time after the Commonwealth right into the present century, many rural churches and chapels made do with a band composed of local musicians.

CHURCH BANDS

These church bands were immortalised by Thomas Hardy in his novel "Under the Greenwood Tree" (1872). His father and grandfather played in the church band at Stinsford, Dorset, and a plan of the west gallery there, showing the positions of the singers and instrumentalists, still survives with Thomas Hardy's autograph on it. His mother first saw his father playing the violin in the Stinsford gallery – "a good-looking young man in blue trousers, a blue swallow-tailed coat, Wellington boots of the old leather kind and a red and black flowered waistcoat".

History came to life in September 1990 when the BBC televised "Songs of Praise" from Puddletown in Dorset, using a band in the church gallery, including the actual violin that had been played by Hardy's father. I had the privilege of playing my ophicleide on that occasion.

The church bands used any instruments which were available in the area. There were usually 3 to 8 players, some with stringed instruments, and some with wind instruments.

GALLERIES

The band rarely played in the aisle, but would play in the nave, or anywhere else where they could find space. In Padstow it was recorded that the minstrels played on the top of the rood-screen, but this must have been rather unusual. In time galleries were specially built for them at the west end of the church. Splendid examples survive in Dorset, and at Minstead in Hampshire, where there is also a tombstone of a serpent-player, with a beautiful carving of a serpent. In Cornwall the Victorian church architects seem to have removed all the galleries. They were usually made of wood, and more or less self-supporting. They were attached to the west wall of the church, and perhaps the back row of pillars, but when they were removed there was scarcely a trace to be seen.

So far we have talked only of churches, but the position in non-conformist chapels was much the same. When John Wesley was alive, only

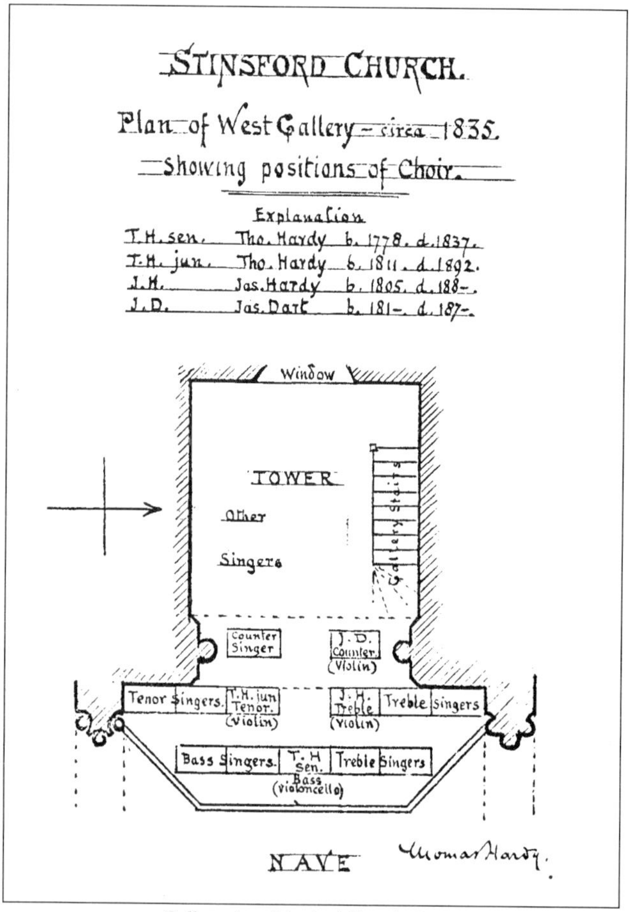

STINSFORD CHURCH.

Plan of West Gallery circa 1835.

Showing positions of Choir.

Explanation

T.H. sen. Tho. Hardy b. 1778. d. 1837.
T.H. jun. Tho. Hardy b. 1811. d. 1892.
J.H.   Jas. Hardy b. 1805. d. 188-.
J.D.   Jas. Dart   b. 181-. d. 187-.

Window

TOWER

Other

Singers

Gallery stairs

Counter Singer

J.D. Counter (Violin)

Tenor Singers. | T.H. jun Tenor. (Violin) | J.H. Treble (Violin) | Treble Singers

Bass Singers. | T.H. sen. Bass (violoncello) | Treble Singers

NAVE

Thomas Hardy.

Gallery plan, Stinsford Church, Dorset.

BBC "Songs of Praise" in Puddletown Church, August 1990.
The Author is playing the ophicleide.

three chapels in England possessed organs. Indeed non-conformist chapels, being built after the Commonwealth, often started their lives with a band.

STANDARDS NOT IDEAL

Reading books on church history makes it clear that the musical standards of the minstrels often left something to be desired. John Chetham, in his book of Psalmody 1724, describes them as "such a wretched mixture of noise and confusion as ought never to be heard in a Christian congregation."

The books are full of anecdotes about the gallery minstrels, who seem to have been most colourful characters.

"John Pennicott lived for forty years in Amberly, (Sussex), where he was bandmaster of the church. He was a clarinet player. On one occasion, through some misunderstanding with the vicar, the bandsmen, although present in church, refused to play. The vicar, who was between eighty and ninety years of age, asked from the pulpit, "Are you going to play or not?" To which Pennicott answered for himself and the bandsmen, "No!" The parson rejoined "Well then, I'm not going to preach", and forthwith came down out of the pulpit in a rage. Later, after the service was over and the parson walked down the village street, the band came out with their instruments and gave him "horn fare", or "rough music", to the vicarage. On another occasion, the same band went out on strike. As they would not play at the service of the church, the vicar called upon all the inns in the village, and was successful in "Freezing the taps", – that is, the landlords agreed not to serve any of the band with liquor. The bandsmen retorted by whitewashing the vicar's windows from top to bottom during the night." (Canon MacDermott).

Imagine my delight when I went to a sale in Par and found a limited edition print of the same Mr Pennicott! It was like history peering out of the picture frame.

Once, in Aldingbourne church, the vicar decided to break a custom by preaching a sermon at matins. The musicians did not like the idea, so when he went up to the pulpit to preach, they started up with the 119th psalm, (the longest of the psalms by far) and simply refused to stop. Eventually the vicar's patience was exhausted, and he left the church to the cheers of the musicians, without delivering his sermon. (Canon MacDermott).

In Exeter cathedral in 1860 the choristers indulged in the little pleasantry of throwing nuts and orange peel on the heads of the congregation. This led to the disuse of the minstrels' gallery.

Kenneth Long had some rather harsh things to say in his book "The Music of the English Church". "If the music was bad, the standard of behaviour was worse, and there seems to have been a total lack of reverence. Instruments would be tuned during the sermon; loud exhortations, blame and praise from the leader of the minstrels would punctuate the service; raucous arguments in the gallery distracted the worshipper

Mr Penniket, Woodmancote Church, Sussex, c.1859.

below; and discussions about the music between the parson, the parish clerk and the leader would be bellowed across the church during the service itself. Some of the instruments were found useful for chastising choirboys, and the intermittent thwacks and the boys' yells were merely another irritation for the congregation to endure".

At St. Neot there is an entry in the church accounts for 1803 "For keeping sentry, i.e. keeping down those who where no singing from the gallery, 1s

A village choir in about 1770.
Print by S H Grimm, London c.1770.

0d". Translated into English, this meant keeping non-singers out of the gallery. One wonders who had this job, and what skirmishes broke out as a result.

The church guide for Liskeard (St. Martin's), tells us that they had "violins, 'cellos, flutes, clarinets, bassoons and SCORPIONS, to make sweet music for the good people of Liskeard". (The "Scorpion" is of course nonsense; there is no such instrument. They might be confusing it with a serpent). Perhaps they were rather irritated by the "scorpions", but in 1832 the "West Briton" newspaper reported "UPROAR IN LISKEARD CHURCH". An extraordinary and disgraceful scene occurred on Easter-day, when the churchwardens tried to refuse entry to the singing-gallery to those who were not on their official list. Two young ladies (or perhaps we should say young women), aided by some young men, forced their way past a churchwarden, and gained seats in the gallery. The desperate struggle was witnessed by the congregation of about a thousand, who themselves took sides in the affair. Yells, hisses, shouts, and even cursing and swearing disturbed the quiet of the Sabbath, and several females were carried out fainting. (This is a summary of a rather long report).

The Sheviock accounts for 1842 complain of the disorderly occupants of the Western gallery.

At Tregrehan chapel in 1862 the choir were sacked for immorality, and asked to return the bass viol.

Nor were the clergy themselves entirely blameless: in 1842 the vicar of St. Breward was "a swearer and drunkard, fined by the mayor of Bodmin, and reprimanded by the Bishop." The rector of Blisland (the adjacent parish), was not a great improvement. He had "lived in concubinage with a cobbler's wife in the village, and had a large family by her, all illegiti-mate". Three centuries earlier, Cardinal Wolsey, as vicar of Lymington, Hampshire, was put in the stocks for being drunk at the village feast.

To be fair to the gallery minstrels, it must be said that then, as now, newspapers and the writers of books (including this one) like a scandal. A good church band playing beautifully would not be newsworthy, and would therefore never attract the attention of the media. To offset the disasters above, there must have been a great many satisfied congrega-tions.

There is very little evidence of disorders in non-conformist chapels, perhaps because the people were more civilised, but possibly because their records are not so well preserved. We do, however, have John Wesley's "Directions for Singing", set out below, which are still relevant today.

WESLEY'S SINGING DIRECTIONS

"Sing **all.** See that you join with the congregation as frequently as you can. Let not the slightest degree of weakness or weariness hinder you. If it is a cross to you, take it up, and you will find a blessing.

Sing **lustily** and with a good courage. Beware of singing as if you were half dead or half asleep; but lift up your voice with strength. Be no more afraid of your voice now, nor more ashamed of its being heard, than when you sung the lays of Satan.

Sing **modestly.** Do not bawl so as to be heard above, or distinct from, the rest of the congregation, that you may destroy the harmony; but strive to unite your voices together so as to make one clear melodious sound.

Sing **in time.** Whatever tune is sung, be sure to keep up with it. Do not run before nor stay behind it; but attend closely to the leading voices, and move therewith as exactly as you can. And take care you sing not too slow. This drawling way naturally steals on all who are lazy; and it is high time to drive it out from among us, and sing all our tunes just as quick as we did at first.

Sing the tunes **as they are.** Many persons acquire a habit of sounding half a dozen notes which are not in the tune for one that is. If able to read music, they would be struck with astonishment at the sight of a tune written as they sing it.

Avoid gurgling. Some persons never sing the notes of the tune at all; but keep up a constant gurgling round about, without ever actually touching them."

Singing lustily and modestly at the same time poses quite a challenge.

THE END OF THE MINSTRELS

By the end of the nineteenth century there were great pressures to get rid of the gallery minstrels. There were many reforming movements in the Church of England to improve the standards of the service generally, but inevitably attention was drawn to the efforts of the gallery minstrels. The preferred solution was the purchase of a pipe organ, but these were expensive, and there was often nobody in the parish who could play one. To solve the latter problem, barrel organs were installed, which required no skill except turning the handle at a constant speed, and ensuring that the popular ditties often provided on the same barrel did not appear during the church service. The cheapest solution was the purchase of a harmonium, or one of its many variants, and these were to be found in churches and chapels all over Cornwall. They were not uni-

A Village choir in the 1840s.

Barrel organ in Wissington Church, Suffolk.

versally liked – at St. Michael Caerhays the parish clerk had his dog in the seat, and at the first note it emitted a long howl.

Here and there a flute or cello continued to play together with a harmonium, but generally speaking the harmonium or organ sounded the death-knell of the gallery minstrels. They were never heard in our churches and chapels again. Although doubtless musical standards were improved, the passing of the gallery minstrels was rather sad, because nearly 200 years of tradition of local amateur musicians was lost almost without trace.

Very few of the old instruments survive – indeed a friend of mine recalls using a boxwood and ivory clarinet to light the fire.

A similar fate befell the manuscript music copied out by the minstrels with such care. Cheap printed hymn books rendered it all obsolete, and no doubt most of it finished up on the fire too.

The best that can be done to bring the minstrels back to life, is to read the records mercifully preserved.

The Author and Alan Tregaskes at St Winnow for the filming of the BBC "Poldark" series.

CHAPTER TWO

THE AUTHOR'S RESEARCH

I was surrounded by music from a very early age. My mother was a pianist with a fine singing voice, and although my father was almost tone-deaf, he was very fond of music, and had a wonderful collection of old 78 records for his acoustic gramophone. I believe he bought the gramophone with coupons from "Craven A" cigarettes. Unfortunately I inherited my father's voice, and not my mother's, and at Carclaze Infants School I used to be sent out on parents' days because my singing spoilt the choir. My mother arranged piano lessons for me, but like many youngsters I rebelled, and would not practise. She insisted that I must learn some instrument, and let me choose my own. This must have been good psychology, because I chose the clarinet, and managed to reach a reasonable standard. Many years later I tried to play the bassoon. After practising for weeks, I proudly played a tune for my father. He listened patiently, then said "I can make a better noise than that without an instrument".

More than twenty years ago a group of friends joined me, and we started playing chamber music for fun, and giving concerts for charity. John Price played the flute, and in recent years played an antique model, and also a beautiful instrument made of ivory. Toni Olsson played the oboe and tenor viol, and Joy McMullen the oboe and cello. Jim Salisbury played the French horn and clarinet, and John Black played the bassoon and vamp horn (see later!). I played the serpent, ophicleide and clarinet.

We had lots of fun and many adventures, and of course over the years raised a lot of money. We played for the BBC several times using our funny old instruments. In the TV studio in Plymouth we played the old hymn "St Austle". With other members of the West Gallery Music Association I played for "Songs of Praise" in Puddletown in Dorset, which included a hilarious barn-dance in the Abbotsbury tithe-barn afterwards. We provided the dance music after the wedding of Dr Ellis and Caroline in the "Poldark" series, with Alan Tregaskes playing the violin, and myself playing the serpent. We spent all day at St Winnow taking part in the filming, with Mr Winston Graham watching, and I missed an important meeting with our Japanese partners at the office. After all that, we only appeared on TV screens for two minutes!

Our wind group gave several concerts on my front lawn which slopes steeply down towards the sea. It was grand for the audience, but the performers used to fall over backwards in their seats, to the merriment of all.

I also play the Swiss alphorn, and on one occasion played it at a concert in a restaurant in St. Austell town centre. The restaurant was on the first floor, and the only way we could get it inside was to pass it through the window over the heads of the diners. St. Austell town centre was brought to a halt by the proceedings! At one of our concerts in Truro Cathedral, we were playing some Bach chamber music as an interlude to poetry readings. One of our pieces was called "Unser Vater", which is "Our Father" in German. Unfortunately the announcer said we would be playing a piece called "Under Water". Ever since we have called it our submarine music. We gave several concerts on Mevagissey quay, where there were two major problems. The audience used to sit on piles of fish-boxes, which always seemed to collapse with a crash just as we reached a quiet passage in the music. The other problem was the seagulls, who used to do their target practice on us, picking especially on the bassoon.

I started giving lecture-recitals on Cornish church and chapel bands in the 1970s, and my friends played the music to illustrate the talks. We

THE OLD CHURCH GALLERY MINSTRELS

in
TREGAMINION CHAPEL OF EASE
on
FRIDAY, 1st OCTOBER, 1982 at 6.30 p.m.
in aid of the
Restoration of the Fabric of TREGAMINION fund

A Talk by **HARRY WOODHOUSE** with music from
THE MID CORNWALL WIND GROUP
Serpent, Ophicleide, Shawm and other surprises

Concert Poster.

14

The Church Gallery Minstrels outside St Austell Church.

The Author and his friends before an "18th century" service in St Winnow Church.

called ourselves the "Old Church Gallery Minstrels". When we started we used to play shawms and a cornett, but they made such a din that people started to walk out, so we changed to more controllable instruments. An unforgettable experience was playing at a re-enactment of a 1779 Prayer Book Evensong service for Canon Miles Brown in St. Winnow church in September 1979. Even the local congregation turned up in period costume.

Since then I have been researching the "Old Church Gallery Minstrels" in Cornwall, with the help of my wife and some of the "Minstrels". After our performances, many people have come to me with tales of their relations who played in church or chapel bands. I gave a short talk on Radio Cornwall, and again it resulted in more information. In 1992 I was greatly honoured to receive a Caroline Kemp Research Scholarship from Exeter University, and had the privilege of working under the direction of Dr Richard McGrady. The research has been published in journals listed in the bibliography, but there was much anecdotal material which was left over, not really suitable for a learned journal! It seemed a shame to waste it, so I have included it in this book.

West Gallery inside Tregaminion Church.

SOURCES

The research started with visits to churches and chapels, but it was soon found that this was a very poor source of information. The only gallery we could find is the one at Tregaminion, Polkerris, near Par, but there is no evidence that it was ever used by minstrels. At Lezant near Launceston, the holes in the granite pillars which supported the west gallery had been neatly plugged with matching granite patches, but no trace of the gallery remained.

Plugged holes from west gallery in Lezant Church.

Evidence for the existence of galleries had to come from church records, and so far we have found 64 churches in Cornwall which had galleries. Not all of them were strongly made – it is said that in 1819 Adam Clarke preached in a St. Austell chapel when the gallery collapsed! Although we have been unable to corroborate this tale, or locate the chapel concerned, John Probert tells me that it is quite likely to be true – Adam Clarke seemed to be accident-prone, and many such stories were associated with his preaching.

Few orchestral instruments are preserved in churches today – those that have survived have been removed to local museums for safety. However, church guides sometimes contain musical information. For example the guide to St. Constantine by Ida and David Fraser Harris (1975), describes the band consisting of an ophicleide and flute, and prints "The Constantine Funeral Hymn" from the nineteenth century. A very large number of church guides are preserved in the Redruth Cornish Studies library, and the Truro Museum library of the Royal Institution of Cornwall. Most churches have had several guides, but often only one of them showed any interest in music.

Visits to museums were very rewarding, and actual musical instruments were found displayed in St. Mary's, Isles of Scilly; Truro; St. Ives, and Launceston, as well as Carharrack and Trewint Methodist Museums. The

Chapel Band instruments in St Mary's Museum, Isles of Scilly.

The Old Chapel, St Mary's, Isles of Scilly where serpent and clarinets were played.

18

Carharrack museum has a 6-keyed boxwood and ivory clarinet by Robert Woly & Co, of London, which used to be played at Garras, St. Mawgan in Meneage, about 1850. There is also a newspaper cutting showing the Webber brothers playing a bassoon and clarinet in a chapel band about 1900, and a good collection of old hymn books. The Trewint museum has an hour glass, which was used to time the sermons, and a picture of the Altarnun Wesleyan choir taken in about 1900, showing a violin and cello, accompanying 15 adult and 4 child singers.

Carharrack Methodist Museum.

By far the best source of information was found to be the old church accounts, "Parish" (DDP) series, preserved in the County Record Office, Truro. Mostly they relate to the routine business of keeping the fabric in repair, but even this is fascinating, and it is very hard to pass over items like "HS for four hunderds of Laughs 2s 2d" in the Altarnun accounts for 1734. Later the same year they bought "A Thousand of Laughs nailes" for 1s 4d. Obviously realising they had problems with the spelling, later entries relate to the purchase of "Laffs". Of course they meant roof laths.

Lanlivery had several entries for "Washing the Surplus". Perhaps they were laundering it in a Swiss bank account? In 1857 they bought "Whine for the Sacrement".

St. Michael Penkevil in 1750 had the entry: "For carrying the Pigeons' Dung out of the Tower and driving it out of the Church-yard 2s 3d".

In the eighteenth century, Tywardreath had many entries for "Burying a corps washed in by the sea", and "Expense on taking up the boddy of a drown'd man at Polredmouth". Such were the obligations of the church in those days.

Horrifying to us today, is the scale of their extermination of "vermin". In 1806 St. Dominic paid for the killing of 1 badger, two fitches (polecats), 4 stoats, 2 hawks, and 31 bullfinches. In 1810 they paid for 3 otters, 6 hedgehogs, and 48 bullfinches. Thank heaven for the RSPCA. Duloe paid for the killing of 4 badgers in 1790. Even in the 1820's, St. Martin-by-Looe was happily paying for the killing of badgers, foxes, hedgehogs, ravens, hawks, stoats, fitches, and kitts (kites, birds of prey once common here).

Of course, we were not supposed to be reading any of this – we were supposed to be researching the gallery minstrels. Sometimes the border-line was not very clear. What, for example, were we to make of a "Bass Scrubber", bought by Perranarworthal church in 1887? We suppose it was a brush. And how about Sheviock in 1821 when they bought "26½ Pounds of Iron Rod for the Conductor", and later paid 7d for "cramps for the con-ducting rod"? It seemed rather a heavy rod for the choir conductor to wield, so we suppose it must have been the lightning conductor. Then there was the "Bear for the Tresmeer singers", who were visiting Egloskerry. We hope they took it home on a lead. We suppose they meant "beer".

There are also chapel records in the County Record Office: their "Methodist Records" (MR) series. Unfortunately these are far from complete, and there are access restrictions on some of them, imposed by the chapel authorities. Sadly, a great many Cornish chapels have fallen into disuse, and their records lost altogether. However, we have studied what records remain, and Mr John Probert of Redruth has kindly allowed us to include in this book some of the results of his researches.

It is a tremendous thrill wading through pages and pages of church records, and suddenly finding an entry like: "For strings for the Base Vile 5s 0d". (Egloskerry, 1804). We have to consider very carefully what we can learn from such church accounts. Clearly they had a "Base Vile" in Egloskerry in 1804. They were probably referring to what we would call a cello. The instrument might have been bought by the church, but if so, there is no record in the accounts. More likely it was a gift from someone in the parish, or perhaps it had been in the player's family for years. Anyway, for some reason the church was buying strings for it, so it must have been played in the church. However, lack of a reference in the accounts might mean many things. An instrument might be played in the church, but it might be owned and maintained by a well-to-do parish-ioner. The church-warden may have recorded it in a way which does not help a historian at all. He may say "Mr Smith's bill 10s 0d." If we are very lucky, we might know that Mr Smith sold musical instruments, but it is not very likely. Finally the accounts may be missing, lost, or destroyed.

It is clear from the above that the references we find must be but a tiny fraction of the total number of instruments which were played in Cornish churches. We have searched 172 sets of church accounts, read hundreds of church guides, read dozens of Cornish history books, and written over 200 pages of notes. Like most scholars, we are still learning. If you, the reader, have any information about church and chapel bands in Cornwall, do please let me know.

Mr Kinnaird-Jenkins in his history of Falmouth church, quotes from a nineteenth-century poet:

"Arrived at the church 'tis diverting to see,

Them all strut to Ned Kendal's vile twiddle dumdee,

Whose bass and whose treble comparatively speaking,

Are like old pigs grunting and little pigs squealing".

From Kenwyn church we found the story of the cello player who said "Give us the rosin, Bill, and I'll let 'em know who's the King of Glory!" At Mullion the cornet player had lost some vital teeth, so he made two wooden ones which he used to stick in his mouth in order to hold his instrument.

Sir Arthur Quiller-Couch tells a splendid story of the minstrels in "The Looe Die-Hards", from his book "Wandering Heath" (1895). The village musicians practised hard for the funeral of one of their colleagues, but to their annoyance he refused to die. This short extract gives the flavour of the marvellous tale:

The French prisoner enquired: "But about this key-bugle, monsieur? And the other instruments? – not to mention the players". "I've been thinking of that", said Captain Pond. "There's Butcher Tregaskis has a key-bugle. He plays 'Rule Britannia' upon it when he goes round with the suet. He'll lend you that until we can get one down from Plymouth. A drum, too, you shall have. Hockaday's trader calls here tomorrow on her way to Plymouth; she shall bring both instruments back with her. Then we have the church musicians – Peter Tweedy, first fiddle; Matthew John Ede, second ditto; Thomas Tripconey, scorpion –" "Serpent", the doctor corrected. "Well, it's a filthy thing to look at, anyway. Israel Spettigew, bass-viol; William Henry Phippin, flute; and William Henry Phippin's eldest boy Archelaus to tap the triangle at the right moment".

A chapel band in Penzance walked out when the organ was installed. Henceforth the place became known as the "organ chapel".

The state of the church fabric often left much to be desired, and did not encourage a spirit of reverence and decorum. Geoffrey Grigson in his book "Freedom of the Parish" (1954) tells us of the state of Pelynt church: "90 years ago the church had fallen into a sad condition. There were

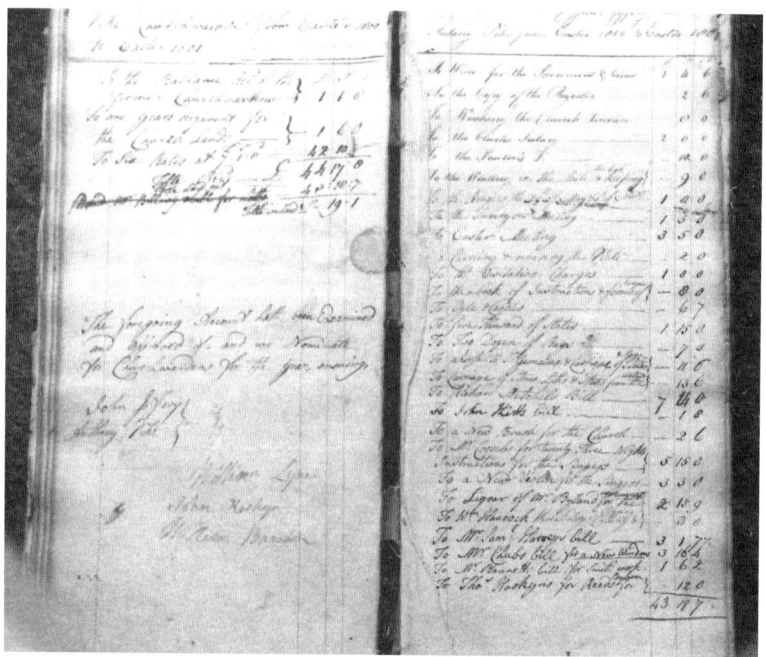

Typical page from a book of church accounts.

holes in the floor, stuffed up with furze faggots. The ruling lady at Trelawne had remarked, I think in opening a bazaar for the restoration fund, that it was pleasant to be surrounded by your ancestors, but less pleasant to smell them through the holes".

Although galleries were built in churches all over Britain, there were rumblings in certain quarters as to their aesthetic qualities. Jonathan Couch in his book "The History of Polperro" (1871) remarks of Lansallos church: "The pulpit and singing-gallery in the nave are of very modern date, and built in the very worst taste". That was nothing compared to the views of the Royal Institute of British Architects. In their transactions (late 19th century) appeared an article "Some Account of the Church of St. Michael Penkevil". It said "As to galleries, when they exist they should be removed, and every architect should resist strenuously their re-erection. Archbishop Laud's opinion is one in which we shall all agree. "The truth is" he says, "I did never like galleries in any church: they utterly deface the grave beauty and decency of those sacred places, and make them look more like a theatre than a church"." This splendid article goes on to explain how important it is to keep dogs out of the chancel. It explains that altar-rails must be kept low (unless the dogs are very well-behaved) to prevent them getting to the altar. We have a dog which comes to our little church in Porthpean on Sundays, but it is very well-behaved. It has not reached the altar yet. In Bangor Cathedral are dog-tongs, formerly used to prevent such happenings.

The delightful spelling of some of the church records has already been mentioned, but we live now in a world dominated by word-processors with spelling checks. Every time I write a letter on mine, it tells me that my name should be spelled "Woodlouse". We must remember though that the first English dictionary was not published until 1721, so that Shakespeare himself did not possess a dictionary.

In 1797 the clerk at Tywardreath was paid £2 10s 0d for "blewing" the oboe. This picturesque word brings to my mind visions of blowing until he was blue. The old form of the cello, "bass viol", offered almost unlimited scope for the unwary scribe. In Cornwall we have found 30 different spellings, including befs viol, bafse voile, bafs violl, base file, baze vial, beais veial, buse viol, base viol, bafs vale, bafs vail, and bafs vaile. No doubt the spelling which best reflected the feelings of the weary churchwarden was "base vile".

As well as queer spellings, we found lots of quaint phrases, like "going after the carpenter" at Bude in 1831. In standard English, this would mean getting him on the job, or "chasing him up"!

When I was a boy, in the 1930s, chapel temperance movements were very strong in the villages, and temperance halls were full. No doubt this was a reaction to some of the excesses in the Church of England in former times.

COSTS OF PROVIDING THE MUSIC

It was not usual to pay the musicians or the singers, but they were rewarded for their efforts by an annual "feast". These are well recorded, and occur in most churches at some time. For example at North Tamerton in 1834: "Malt and hops for the singers £1 2s 0d". It appears that this was a sort of do-it-yourself feast: they had to brew their own beer. The accounts at Egloskerry in 1787 are a little more specific: "For two barrels of Malt and Hops for singers £1 1s 10d", "Ditto 25lbs of beef at 6s 3d, Tea etc 2s 0d: 12s 4d". One wonders how much beer two barrels of malt would make. All is revealed at North Tamerton in 1773 where the singers drank "20 gallands of sider 20s 0d". The St. Giles' singers were visiting at the time, but even if there were forty musicians present this would still be four pints each. At Egloskerry in 1799 we find "For Bread and candles when the singers drink the cyder 4s 5½". At least they did not do it in darkness. At Jacobstow in 1792 we find "A pock of whoats for the same 2s 6d. Paid for Shuger and Tay and iggs, corrants and candles do 2s 4d. For 2 pounds of Botter 1s 0d, 3 pints of crome 1s 3d, do 2s 3d". It appears that the church warden had not fully recovered when he wrote the accounts.

At Helland in 1763: "Paid for a healfe a houfged of Sidder £1 10s 0d". (Hav anouther dhrinc).

All these jollifications were quite expensive for the church. For example at St. Antony in 1824, the church's annual expenditure was £39 2s 5½, and of that £15 2s 5d (39%) was spent on the singing master, instrumentalists and the singers' meeting. In modern times this would be equivalent to about £1330 and £514 respectively.

DRINK!

Drink seems to figure prominently in most church accounts. For example at St. Stephens by Saltash in 1847: "21 quarts of wine and bread for seven Sacraments £1 10s 0d". If there were 20 communicants this would imply that when each one went up to the communion table the vicar gave him two glasses of wine. At one church up in England, such a communicant is alleged to have said "The Very Good Health of Our Lord Jesus Christ!" At Zennor in 1772 we find: "A pint of Brandy to kill a calf 1s-0d". Perhaps they drowned it? At Duloe in 1778 we have: "For 2 bottles of Brandy for the Survey of the Tower 2s 10½". Perhaps it was to fill the spirit level on the surveying instrument? One church bought brandy, gin and rum by the gallon, quart, pint, and noggin. Another, which had better be nameless, or I might have to go into hiding, bought a gallon of Canary for the Easter celebrations in the early 19th century. The following year it was 2 gallons. Then it was 3 gallons, then 4 gallons. Just when I could not believe things could get any worse, I found the entry "£1 1s 0d for girls". No more feasts were recorded after this.

At Egloskerry in 1802 we found the entry: "For the Incorrigement to the Young Men that Play the Music 5s 0d". We hope the young men were suitably incorriged, but fear they probably spent the money on beer. At North Petherwin in 1794 we found: "For rewarding the singers and incorrigonant for the singers to be gave in a treat £1 1s 0d".

SMUGGLING

There were even worse excesses up in England. In Broadstairs (Kent) when a cargo of smuggled goods was expected the clerk would go to the top of the spire, from which he had a splendid view, and when the coast was clear of preventive men he would give the signal by hoisting the church flag. A clergyman, at this period, arriving one Sunday at a small church, where he held services on alternate Sundays, was informed by the clerk that there would be no service that day.

Upon asking the reason he was told, "The pulpit be full of tea and the vestry wi' brandy".

John Probert tells the story of a lecture at Lanner Wesleyan Guild to be given by Mr A.K.Hamilton-Jenkin. The preacher opened the devotions and thanked God for sending Mr Jenkin all that way with a message to make them better men and women to go into the world to make it a better place. However, Mr Jenkin's lecture was about smuggling and wrecking.

Enough of all this: let us look now at the instruments the gallery minstrels were playing.

CHAPTER THREE

THE INSTRUMENTS

In the sixteenth century there are references to instruments other than the organ being played in church, but the references are rather unhelpful, such as "and other excellent musicall instruments". For special occasions the town waits (described later) would play their instruments in church, but they were really more suitable for out-door performances. The most popular instruments were trumpets and shawms (precursors of the oboe). Sackbuts and cornetts were then added. The sackbut was an early trombone, and the cornett (not to be confused with the modern cornet, or the ice-cream variety) was an early woodwind instrument played with a cup-mouthpiece. These wind instruments were joined by stringed instruments of the viol family, and the violin itself. Violins were played in church for the funerals of Queen Elizabeth and King James I. King Charles I engaged 24 "violins" to play in the Chapel Royal. He had enjoyed the gracious music of the French court, and wanted to hear the same sort of sound in his own chapel. "Violins" included violas and cellos as well; in fact it was what we would call a string orchestra today.

For the "gallery minstrel" period after the Commonwealth we are on firmer ground, and several researchers have published lists of the instruments used. Canon MacDermott published his list in 1948: violin, flute, clarinet, violoncello (often called the bass-viol), bassoon, trombone, oboe, cornet, serpent, double-bass, ophicleide, cornopean, fife, baritone, cross-blown flageolet, flutina, concertina, banjo, bass-horn, French-horn, Kent-bugle, vamp-horn, pitch-pipe, and triangle. These were as far as possible in order of their frequency of use. In 1970 Lyndesay Langwill and Canon Boston produced a book on "Church and Chamber Barrel-Organs", which contains a list of church band instruments from all over Britain. This list adds the accordion, bass flute, and tenor oboe. The only Cornish reference is "Feock – said to have seven bassoons?" Professor Temperley published his book "The Music of the English Parish Church" in 1979. This masterly work also contains a list of instruments used from 1742 to 1785.

In Cornwall we have found references to the following instruments, but no others. Bass-viol (cello), violin, flute, clarinet, bassoon, oboe, serpent, ophicleide, double-bass, cornet, bass-horn, fife, trombone, and keyed bugle. Again these are in order of frequency of occurrence in the records. The full list is shown in the appendix, together with dates and places of occurrence.

It is clear that our list must represent only a tiny fraction of the total number of instruments once used in Cornwall. It is highly likely that most churches and chapels in Cornwall had a band at some time.

Most instruments were bought new, but there are many references to the purchase of second-hand instruments in Cornwall, and even exchanging a bassoon for a bass viol. At St. Minver in 1836 they paid for "half a bass viol". One imagines that somebody else must have paid half the cost. It would be very difficult to play half a bass viol, even if it were the top half.

One thing all the old wind instruments had in common, was that they were very difficult to play in tune. My group of friends have been struggling for years to play in tune, and every time we replay a recording of a rehearsal, we groan inwardly. Even if we tune to a standard "A", all the other notes seem to go wrong. For example, the antique flute goes sharp as it goes higher, and the boxwood and ivory clarinet goes flat. What is the use of tuning to an "A" on the serpent, when every note can be moved up or down three or four notes just by changing the lip-pressure?

PITCHPIPE

The first instrument encountered in the Cornish records is often a "pitchpipe", usually in the early eighteenth century. The earliest one we found mentioned in Cornwall was in 1760. It consisted of a whistle with a plunger at the bottom, rather like a small stopped organ pipe, or an American "Swannee whistle". It was used by the leader of the singers to set the pitch for the singing, when there was no band or organ. There are numerous anecdotes of disasters, when somebody accidentally (or on purpose) knocked in the plunger, setting the singers far too high. All would go well until a high note came, beyond the reach of the singers. Contemporary singing books gave dire warnings of incorrect pitching of tunes, causing them to go beyond the range of the voices, and producing "squeaking above, or grumbling below".

Maker church had a pitchpipe 2ft long and 1½ inches wide with a different note at each end. The singers had their own gallery where the vestry now is, until the restoration of 1874. They also had a flute, and probably other instruments too, but these were replaced first by a harmonium, and then by an organ in 1875.

We were surprised to find that tuning-forks were used in Cornish churches. They were bought by Madron in 1814, Forrabury in 1831, and Poughill in 1861. The tuning fork was invented in 1711 by Handel's trumpeter, John Shore, and until recent times was the most accurate means of establishing pitch. However, the tuning fork was very expensive, and factory-made. The humble pitchpipe was cheap, and could be home-made by a village carpenter.

STRINGS.

There is little to say about the string family of instruments, because they were basically the same as the instruments we know today. Centuries ago there was a whole family of viols, but these became almost obsolete before the days of the gallery minstrels. It is interesting that our modern double-bass still retains the shape of the old viol family, with its sloping shoulders and flat back, although it was not an original member of the family. For some strange reason the violoncello, or cello, was nearly always referred to by the minstrels as a "bass viol", with sundry spelling variants as already mentioned.

Even the violin was not immune to being mis-spelt. Poughill has VYLING and VILIN, and Poundstock has VIROLIN (Virol builds healthy children I seem to remember).

The Rev F.W.Galpin founded the Galpin Society, which specialises in the study of old musical instruments. He wrote several books, and was very interested in church bands. In an article of 1905 entitled "Notes on the Old Church Bands and Village Choirs of the Past Century", he explains that the Winterborne band in Dorset did not have a violin "due to the wishes of the parson, who shared the once general opinion that it "savoured of the public-house".

An address delivered to the Society of Singers of Llanberis, Wales in 1827 contained this statement: "Such instruments as telyn (harp), bass and viol are unnatural to God and to the worship of Him. To play with the fingers on the strings is more fitting for satisfying the drunkard when he is in his wine than to use such for worshipping a Spiritual Being". Why fingers on strings are more wicked than fingers on the keys of a woodwind instrument I do not know. And what about King David and his harp?

Believe it or not, violins and cellos were sometimes made by a local blacksmith out of metal. Langwill and Boston reported that they had found that metal cellos had been used in Barsham and Mattishall Burgh in Norfolk. Canon MacDermott mentioned copper bass-viols in Bosham and Eastbourne, and one made of sheet-iron in Devizes museum (it is still there). The John Moore Quire have recently borrowed a sheet steel cello from Stoke City museum. Here in Cornwall we have a "tin" violin preserved in excellent condition in Truro museum. We do not know if it was ever played in church, but the museum description reads as follows: "This violin was made about 1850 by a Redruth tinsmith of tinned iron sheet. Traditionally it was fashioned after the original wooden sound-box had fallen apart when filled with hot rum by lively sailors. The violin has a surprisingly sweet tone. It was used for playing sea-shanties and is said to have been retrieved once from a sinking ship".

The first gallery minstrel? King David playing the harp
(From "The Whole Book of Psalms" by John Playford).

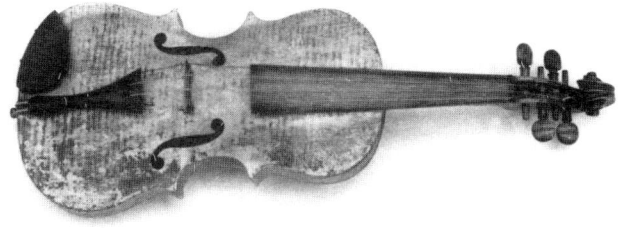

Tin violin, Truro Museum.

T. Thomas of Trispen playing his bass viol.

31

FLUTE

The flute shared with the violin second place in popularity in Cornish churches after the cello. "Flute" in the gallery minstrel context always meant the transverse or "German" flute; the recorder or "flute-a-beck" was never found in a church. Today the flute is usually made of metal, although it is still referred to as a "woodwind" instrument. A hundred and fifty years ago flutes were usually made of boxwood and ivory, with just one brass key at the bottom for D sharp. Much boxwood was grown in England at the time: nowadays it is quite rare and I import mine from the Middle East. Boxwood survives quite well the repeated wetting and drying inherent in a wind instrument, but in the longer term it has a nasty tendency to warp and twist. Occasionally ivory flutes were played in churches, but these must have been very rare and expensive. The layman might feel that having only one key would make the flute easier to play, but of course the snag is that it is very difficult to get it in tune, especially in a cold damp church. The modern metal Boehm flute has dozens of keys, and the holes are scientifically placed to produce all the notes in tune.

Canon MacDermott says that the flute was often used to wallop small choirboys. This could not have improved its intonation, nor endeared it to the boys.

The bass flute is twice the length of the ordinary flute, and produces a gorgeous soft breathy sound an octave lower. Very little classical music is written for it, but it is often heard today in films and TV background music. I would have thought it would be almost inaudible in a church band. I had one for many years, but its cost was out of all proportion to the opportunities for playing it.

The fife is a small flute frequently played in military bands together with drums. Its tone must have been rather piercing in church. Fifes are still often to be found in Cornish antique shops.

The flutina is no relation of the flute, but a sort of cross between an accordion and a concertina. None of my music text-books has heard of it – not even the great Grove's Dictionary of Music and Musicians, but it is described in Canon MacDermott's book.

The cross-blown flageolet is equally obscure. Apparently it was a flageolet (something like a recorder, often with keys) with its mouthpiece at right angles to its body.

CLARINET

T he early clarinets were made of boxwood, with ivory rings to stop the
ends from cracking. They had five or more keys, but every maker
produced a slightly different system – mine has no key for F natural,
which presents rather a challenge when playing in flat keys. Modern
Boehm system clarinets are made of blackwood, or plastic for student's
models, with a very complicated system of keywork. Although it looks

The author playing his boxwood and ivory clarinet.

complicated, as with the flute it is much easier to play in tune than the old instruments with few keys. The clarinet has a single reed made of a special sort of cane, and years ago it used to be tied onto the ebony mouthpiece with string. Nowadays it is fixed with a metal ligature. Most woodwind instruments sound an octave higher if the player blows a bit harder, and opens a key at the top of the instrument. The clarinet however behaves like a stopped organ pipe, and sounds one and a half octaves higher. This makes the fingering a bit harder to learn, but the main snag is that if the player does not get his lip-pressure, or embouchure, exactly right, it makes the most awful screech. It tries to play a note which is not in the scale of the music, or indeed not music at all. Living with a learner on the clarinet is just one stage better than living with an aspiring violin player.

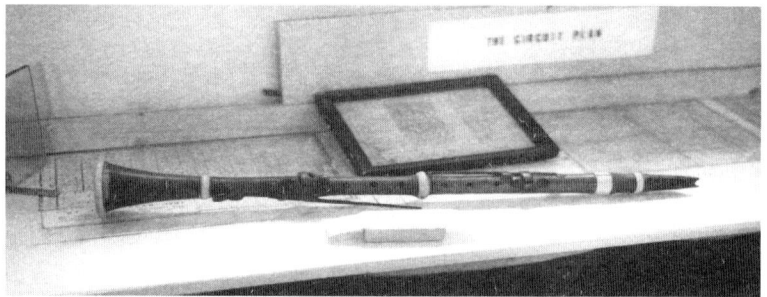

Boxwood and ivory clarinet in a Cornish Museum, formerly played in a Wesleyan Chapel.

In his book "The City", Charles Lee wrote a chapter "The Portrait of a Cornish Musician". In it he says: "When a clarinet "cowked", or made the harsh sound incident to reed instruments when moisture fails them, the player would stamp down the gallery, go outside, and dip his reed in the stream that flowed past the church gate". We know from other accounts that the anecdote refers to St. Mawgan in Pydar church. The stream still flows just below the church gate, but why the player did not simply moisten the reed in his mouth, I do not know. Perhaps leaving the church was an excuse for a quick slurp from the hip-flask.

My good friend Dr Kenneth Phillipps gave me another tale of St. Mawgan in Pydar, from Charles Lee's journal. "Jan 4th 1903. Old John James's account of the choir in the old days, when the music was supplied by two flutes, two clarinets, and a bass viol, who, when the Parson announced "Let us sing, etc." sounded in succession the notes of the common chord from top to bottom......And how, on one occasion, when the musicians were not there (and usually, in that case, the parson would omit the instruction to sing, but the gallery was dark and he near-sighted and he made a mistake) the only minstrel present being Landlord Gilbert... and three or four boys, Gilbert rose to the occasion, stood up, and chanted: Ha-Ha-Ha-Ha" (To the common chord of B flat).

Canon MacDermott can be relied on to find a good story, and sure enough, he tells us of a young singer in Bosham, Sussex. If he stopped singing for a moment, the clarinettist would thrust the bell of his instrument into the lad's ear and blow a shrill and mighty blast to urge him to renewed effort. What the congregation thought of this is not recorded.

OBOE

The oboe, or "hautboy", or "hobo" is similar in size to the clarinet, but has a slim conical bore and is played with a small double reed of cane. It started life as a raucous shawm played out-doors by the town

St Mawgan in Pydar Church, with stream in foreground.

waits, but was tamed by giving it a smaller reed between the player's lips instead of being uncontrolled inside the mouth. In 1800 it had only one key like the early flutes, but keys were gradually added to improve the intonation and make it easier to play. The oboe has a smaller range than the clarinet, and produces a more strident, but somehow plaintive, sound. Fortunately it does not screech like the clarinet. For once MacDermott fails us, and he has no funny jokes about the oboe. For many years I had a boxwood oboe with one key, by the famous maker George Astor. Unfortunately the top joint had split rather badly, but I had repaired it by running beeswax into the crack. (The Galpin Society rather frowns on repairs involving *Superglue*). All went well for many years, until my friend Joy McMullen played it with our group in the Plymouth television studios. The high intensity lights melted the beeswax with disastrous results.

The tenor oboe is a little longer than the oboe, and in the 18th century was used in military bands. Over the years makers produced it in several different shapes; in more recent times it turned into the cor anglais, which means English horn (quite a good name really except that it is neither English nor a horn). It has a bulbous bell at the bottom, and Hoffnung produced a marvellous cartoon showing one laying an egg. It is surprising that such a rare and valuable instrument should turn up in a church band.

John Wells, of Lindfield, Sussex playing a bassoon.

BASSOON

The bassoon is a bass oboe, and is made (almost) manageable by doubling the tube back on itself. In the hands of a good player it produces a delicious soft buzzing sound, and is very well suited to supporting the singers' bass line. In the Poundstock accounts for 1789 we find: " Singing Master and Strings for the Bafsoon, £1 6s 0d". My friend John Black who has played the bassoon all his life said "Good Heavens! Nobody ever told me I had to fit strings". Churchwardens often seemed vague on the subject of bassoons, and in the history of Talland parish, Frank Perrycoste says "possibly the bassoon in question was a bass viol". For some strange reason the public often laugh when the bassoon is played. Possibly its name is rather reminiscent of "buffoon". St. Winnow had a new "Bassone" in 1805. The mind boggles. The bassoon normally has a wooden "bell" joint (the piece that sticks up at the end) but several with metal bells have been reported in churches over the years. I found one which had belonged to Rilla Mill chapel, having a metal bell as a replacement for its normal wooden one.

Rilla Mill Chapel where a bassoon was played.

Canon MacDermott tells us that St. Feock church once had seven bassoons, and "when they all played the bass and closed down on low F it was like heaven". It seems a shame to question such a lovely story, but we have spent ages trying to find confirmation in the Cornish records. Certainly in 1839 the Feock accounts show the purchase of "An old bassoon 5s 0d", but unfortunately most of the Feock accounts have gone missing. They bought a keyed bugle in 1836, so the band could not have been just bassoons then. Few people today can have heard the sound of

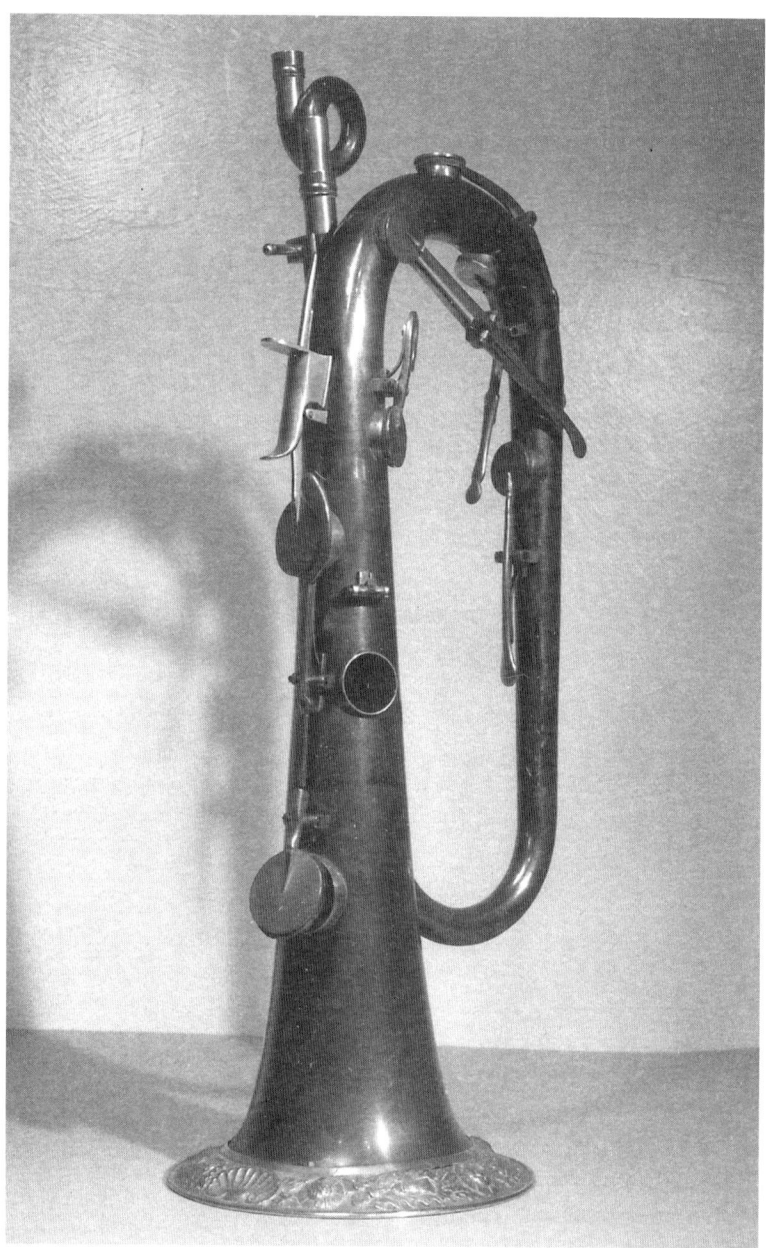

Keyed bugle.

seven bassoons playing a hymn, so in my lecture-recitals my daughter plays six bassoons superimposed on a tape recording, and John Black plays the seventh part "live". To everyone's amazement, it makes a really beautiful sound.

Canon MacDermott goes on to say that Alfriston church had five bassoons, and Brightling had nine ("in order to drown the choir")! Since these are up in England, (both in Sussex), they have not been covered by our researches.

OBSOLETE WOODWIND

S tudents of orchestration today are told about woodwind instruments which produce their sound with reeds or by blowing across a hole, whereas brass instruments have a cup mouthpiece like the trumpet, French horn, and trombone. The player makes a raspberry with his lips against the rim of the mouthpiece, and with luck a beautiful sound comes out the other end.

There was once a family of instruments combining both ideas – now sadly all obsolete. The cornett, keyed bugle, lysarden, serpent, bass-horn, and ophicleide all have cup mouthpieces like a brass instrument, and bodies with holes in the sides like a flute.

CORNETT

T he cornett was the highest sounding member of the family. It was used by Monteverde (1567-1643) in his Vespers, but was obsolete long before the time of the gallery minstrels.

KEYED BUGLE

T he keyed bugle was patented by Joseph Halliday in 1810. It was an ordinary military bugle but with holes in the sides covered by pads contained in brass keys. The Dublin maker Matthew Pace seems to have made the first keyed bugle, which became known as the Royal Kent Bugle as a compliment to H.R.H. the Duke of Kent (then Commander-in-Chief of the British Army). The ordinary bugle can only play bugle-calls. The keyed bugle was able to fill in the gaps between the bugle-calls and play proper tunes. However, Cecil Forsyth's textbook on orchestration tells us that it was shockingly defective in intonation. In Cornwall we found a keyed bugle in the Feock records, as already mentioned.

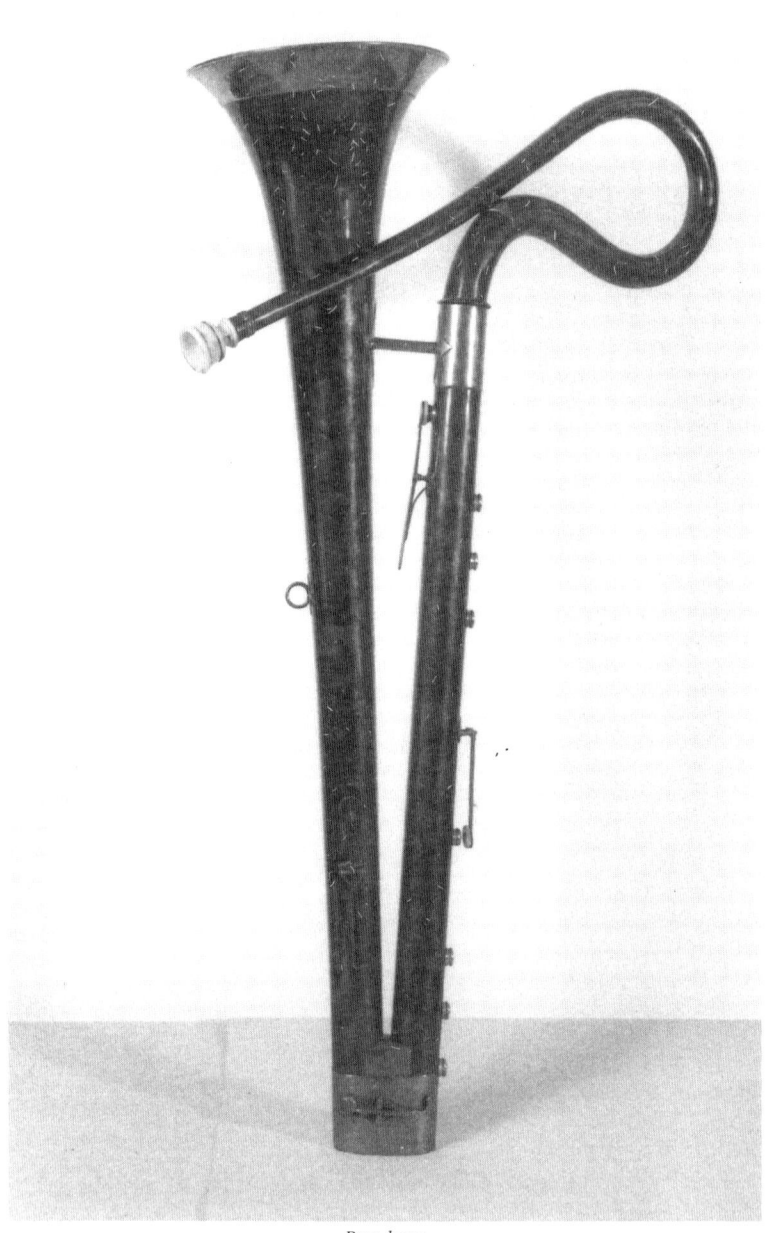

Bass-horn.

SERPENT

Even more defective in every way was the serpent, said to have been invented by a Canon of Auxerre in France in 1590. Although it is obsolete, there are several antique specimens in museums, and even a few not in captivity. I have one myself which I play in my lecture recitals. Modern replicas are still being made, and the fibreglass version can be heard every week in the summer in the Isles of Scilly at Roger Smith's early music concerts.

The serpent has a wooden tube about eight feet long, coiled onto itself in serpentine fashion – hence of course the name. The tube is actually carved in sections to follow the grain of the wood, and the bits are all glued together and bound with bandages like an Egyptian mummy. The whole contraption is finally bound with black leather. Six fingerholes are provided, often lined with ivory, and there are a variable number of rather ineffective brass keys. The serpent is fitted with a brass sliding tube (laughably referred to as the tuning tube) and a large cup mouthpiece with thin walls, often made of ivory. Very few were made in factories – they were usually made by an enthusiastic amateur or the local village carpenter. Consequently they are all different, and even need different fingering systems.

The serpent was originally invented to accompany plainsong in French churches, but about the middle of the eighteenth century it appeared in German bands, and spread into military bands all over Europe. In England it was played in churches and in bands, and the military version often had its bell turned slightly outwards. This great invention(!) is credited to King George III, and was said to make the thing easier to play on the march. It was customary to paint the inside of the bell red, and I often wondered why this was done. My friend Roger Smith provided the answer, removing his tongue from his cheek from time to time. The army used to send the serpent player in front of the advance, and the enemy, on hearing the sound, would immediately shoot the serpent player. You can hardly blame them. The red paint inside the bell prevented the blood from showing.

Nobody today really knows what the serpent sounded like in the hands of a virtuoso player. We do know that it was extremely difficult to play, because the wide tube makes it possible to lip any note several semitones up or down, and the fingerholes are far too small, and all in the wrong places acoustically. The keys are of little help either, and the large flat leather pads tend to leak and make things worse. For any player of a modern woodwind instrument, the fingering is a nightmare. Since the beast is held with right and left hands on opposite "limbs" of the serpent, the fingering of the right hand is backwards. It is possible to play a descending scale on the serpent, while fingering it for an ascending scale and vice versa. It is the custom today to make fun of the serpent, and play

The Author playing his serpent for the BBC "History of the English Carol".

motorbike noises on it, but when played properly it makes a beautiful soft woody sound, which blends with voices very well.

Canon MacDermott tells us that some of the English clergy objected to the use of the serpent in divine worship on the grounds that it was unscriptural. It is certainly true that the serpent is not mentioned in the Bible as a musical instrument (although it did tempt Eve), but the same could be said of the bassoon and the clarinet. Perhaps they are unscriptural too. In the graveyard at Minstead, Hampshire, is a tombstone with a beautiful carving of a serpent on it. The inscription says: "To the memory of Thomas Maynard who departed this life July 9th, 1807, aged 27 years". The monument was erected by the Band of Musicians of the 8th Hants Yeomanry, of which Maynard was a member, and he perhaps played his serpent in the quaint old church at Minstead, which still has a minstrels' gallery. Ever since seeing this, my wife has been reading Cornish tombstones, trying to find a poem about a gallery minstrel. She has not yet been successful, but we know of another poem on a grave in Warnham, near Horsham, Sussex:

"His duty done, beneath this stone

Old Michael lies at rest,

His rustic rig, his song, his jig

Were ever of the best.

With nodding head the choir he led,

That none should start too soon;

The second too, he sang full true,

His viol played the tune.

And when at last his age had passed,

One hundred, less eleven,

With faithful cling to fiddle string,

He sang himself to heaven."

Despite its many shortcomings, the serpent had music written for it by Handel, Wagner, Berlioz and Mendelssohn, and indeed I have played the serpent part in the last's "A Calm Sea and a Prosperous Voyage" with the Cornwall Symphony Orchestra. In July 1990 every serpent player in the world was invited to play at a concert in St John's, Smith Square, London, to commemorate the 400th anniversary of the invention of the serpent. About 80 serpent players turned up, and there was standing room only for the congregation, or perhaps I should say audience. Amongst other works we played "The Elephant" from Saint-Saen's "Carnival of the Animals", and Tchaikowsky's "1812" Overture, with the audience bursting balloons instead of firing cannon.

We have found references to thirteen serpents in Cornwall, between 1799 and 1860, and met a man whose grandfather made a serpent (and a harmonium!) for Breage church in about 1860. Breage church had box-pews then. My serpent came from the chapel at the top of the hill in Rilla Mill. It was found in an attic still in its green baize bag.

There is a serpent in the museum in St. Mary's, Isles of Scilly, with a notice which says it was played in the old chapel there in the 1830s.

If you think I am slightly dotty about the serpent, you are absolutely right. My Cornish Bardic name is "Gwaryer an Sarf", or the serpent player.

About half the size of a serpent, the lysarden was a tenor cornett, and bent into a gentle S shape. As far as I know it has never been found in a church band.

John Probert has a most interesting entry in his book "The Worship and Devotion of Cornish Methodism". He states that Lanner Wesleyan chapel paid 15s 7½d towards a serpent in 1857, and before 1889 they had a flute, serpent and "horselegs", which Mr Probert describes as a wind instrument with a bent end. "Horselegs" does not appear in any of my textbooks on musical instruments, but I think it must be a nickname for a bass-horn, which would certainly fit this description. (See page 40).

Several people had a go at improving the serpent, and goodness knows there was plenty of room for improvement. The bass-horn was a kind of upright serpent invented by L.A.Frichot in the 1790's. It had two sections of metal tube, usually of copper, fixed together at an acute angle. The large end was fitted with a huge flared metal bell; the small end had a long graceful swan-necked crook. Three or four keys were usually fitted. It was a much more convenient shape to play than the serpent, and was said to have had a more powerful tone. An excellent example can be seen in the Horniman Museum, Forest Hill, London. Although it must have looked very modern at the time, it still had most of the shortcomings of the serpent, so did not survive long. Canon MacDermott had only heard of one in a church in the whole of England, and that was at Heathfield, Sussex. We were delighted to find one in the church records for Ludgvan in 1856, as well as the mention by Mr Probert about Lanner chapel.

OPHICLEIDE

A more radical redesign of the serpent was carried out by Halary in France in 1821, and he called his instrument the "Ophicleide", or

Mr Kessell with his Grandfather's ophicleide
(Played at Trenoweth Chapel, Mabe c1880).

The Author with his ophicleide.

keyed snake in Greek. It consisted of a conical brass tube, doubled back on itself like a bassoon, fitted with a crook and brass keys operated by levers. While the fingerholes of the serpent were too small, and all in the wrong place, the ophicleide had acoustically designed holes of the right size and position. It was played with a brass cup mouthpiece. The improved keywork made the ophicleide much easier to play in tune; the tone was louder and more even throughout its compass. There were two snags: the fingering was irrational and quite hard to learn, and the keywork was so complicated and fragile that the slightest knock (like the player falling off his horse in a military band) would render it unplayable. There was a further snag which the inventor could not have foreseen. Brass instruments with valves were invented in 1815, and the tuba rapidly made the ophicleide obsolete. The tuba was much easier to play, and much more robust.

Mendelssohn scored for the ophicleide in the Overture to "Midsummer Night's Dream", although nowadays it is always played on the tuba. I had the honour of playing my ophicleide in Mendelssohn's "Elijah" with the St. Austell Choral Society. There are several tutors for the ophicleide, all in French. Judging by their illustrations, you need to have a large moustache to play it properly. Older readers may remember that there was an angel playing the ophicleide in the frieze on the front cover of "Punch".

Frieze from the front cover of "Punch" 1913.

We have found records of five ophicleides in Cornwall between 1860 and 1880. Indeed there are two in Cornwall still. The records show they were played at Constantine, Edgcumbe Methodist Chapel (near Falmouth), Hellesveor, Tregajorran Chapel, and Trenoweth Chapel (Mabe). The last miraculously came to light recently. Following a talk I gave on Radio Cornwall, a farmer from near Newquay phoned me to say he had a strange brass instrument in his loft, wrapped in a green baize bag. It had been played in Trenoweth Chapel by his grandfather, who died in 1943 aged about 70. He brought it to my house, where I told him it was an ophicleide, and played him a tune on it. It was in superb condition – just like new.

It is generally considered that the serpent gave way to the ophicleide about 1860, and an old photograph of the Tregajorran Chapel band and choir taken about that date shows both a serpent and an ophicleide.

I have an ophicleide too. We had a family holiday in France, and returned to Cherbourg on the last Sunday to catch our ferry back to Southampton. My wife had gone to bed early with a headache, and I went wandering round the town, where I saw a very battered ophicleide in a junk shop. The shop was of course closed, but I asked the neighbours where the owner lived. I went to his house to find that he was in bed, but he put his dressing-gown on and came to the shop in his pyjamas. He showed me the ophicleide, for which he wanted £35. My limited French was severely taxed – my phrase book did not have useful phrases like "How much is the ophicleide in the window?". I was hardly in a good position to haggle, and had no money with me. I went back to my wife, who was now asleep, and woke her up. She gave me all our remaining

Tregajorran Choir and Band about 1860.

cash, exactly £35. I bought the ophicleide, but my long-suffering family had nothing to eat on the ferry because we had no money left. The instrument was in a very bad state, but I rebuilt it in my workshop, and have been playing it ever since.

The trombone, cornet, baritone, and French horn require no description, since they were almost identical to instruments used today. The conopean was an early form of cornet with only two valves. Similarly the concertina, accordion, banjo and triangle need no explanation.

VAMPHORN

This can certainly not be said of the vamphorn. Sadly, we have not found records of one being used in a church in Cornwall, but it was one of Canon MacDermott's favourites. They seem to have been quite common in Sussex. They were not really musical instruments at all, but huge tinplate megaphones from three to seven feet long. The "player" sang or shouted into the vamp-horn, and a magnified version came out from the other end. Canon MacDermott lists the various uses of the vamp-horn: to call the cattle home, to call the people from the fields to the services in the church, to summon assistance in time of danger, to give out the psalms and hymns in church, to augment the voice of the clerk, for one of the singers to sing bass through it, to supply a missing part to the band, to reinforce the voice of the celebrant at High Mass in the Middle Ages, to enunciate the bass notes without any attempt at pro-

Vamp-horn at East Leake, Notts.

Huers' horns, Newquay.

nouncing the words, to give forth the tune before singing, for "Precenting", for shouting, to rouse labourers in the morning and call them home at night, for a signal to gleaners to begin or leave off work, by the parish clerk to announce events. It is hard to see how we can manage today without it.

A friend has pointed out to me the similarity to the Cornish instrument used by the huers to announce the arrival of pilchards. There are well-known "huers' houses" on the cliffs at Newquay and St.Ives, and some of the actual instruments are preserved in Cornish museums, including one in the Truro Museum. The instruments seem identical to the pictures of vamphorns in Sussex. I am sure my friend is right, and who knows, the same instrument could easily have been used in a Cornish church.

A related instrument was the Cornish "May Horne", used in the jollifications on May Day. This seems to have been a real musical instrument, not just a megaphone. My wife remembers hearing them played in

Mrs Jacquie Clarke playing the Ashurst vamp-horn.

Newlyn in the early 1930s, just before they became obsolete. It would be most interesting to know if they too were used in churches or chapels.

We made a vamphorn out of cardboard, and used it in a concert in Truro. We shall not do it again. Our bassoon player sang the bass part through it, but could not hear the sound that came out of the other end (fortunately for him). We could, and promptly had hysterics.

"May Hornes" for sale at 6d each outside a Penzance shop, circa 1920.

During my researches on the Cornish bagpipes I came across a reference to bagpipes being played in a Scottish Church. It never seems to have happened south of the border.

In the accounts for the church at St. Clement is an entry for the purchase of a "Buzaglio". We racked our brains as to what on earth this was, and thought it must have been some kind of horn (Latin buculus meaning young bullock), or else the trade name of an Italian organ manufacturer. Mr Douch of the Truro Museum came to our aid, and he discovered it was an Italian heating stove! Shortly afterwards the church started ordering coal.

BARREL-ORGAN

Having dealt with the "inorganic" instruments *(see footnote)*, we must look briefly at the instruments of the organ family which supplanted them. Often the first arrival was a barrel-organ, which was an ordinary pipe-organ with a barrel instead of a keyboard to admit wind to the pipes.

(footnote: I apologise for the Author's sense of humour. He was an inorganic chemist. He means here "not organ!" Ed.)

Small headless nails or "pins" were driven into the wooden barrel, and as the barrel turned the pins moved levers which admitted air to the pipes. It was not usual to provide a complete set of pipes, but just enough for playing hymns in simple keys. I have a Flight and Robson church barrel organ which has drums, triangle and cymbal and seven ranks of pipes but no B flats or E flats. It can only play in sharp keys. It was bought at a church sale in Stoke-on-Trent by my uncle for 5s 0d, and given to another of my uncles as a joke. He sent the pipes away for cleaning, but

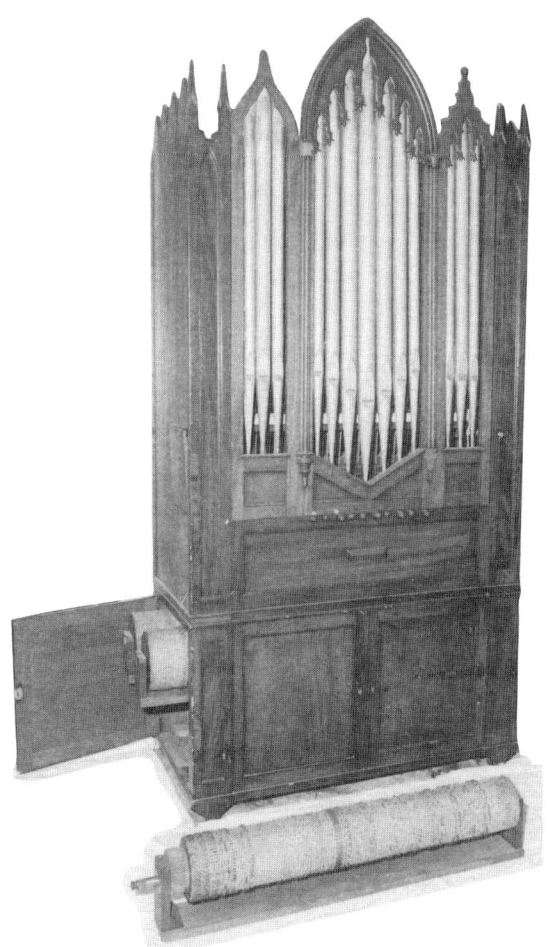

The Author's church barrel organ.

Shelland barrel organ played by Robert Armstrong 1885-1935.

sadly they all got lost, and the organ stood forlornly in his garage for years and years. When uncle died, the organ was going to be given to the dustmen, but instead I sent a Pickfords van to collect it and bring it down to Cornwall.

This organ has three barrels of mixed sacred and secular tunes, and this was quite a common arrangement. The organ often served in the local pub during the week, then was taken to church on Sunday to play the hymns. It is not surprising that occasionally there were accidents. The redoubtable Canon tells us that the barrel-organ in Berwick church had clockwork for its motive power, and on one occasion instead of stopping at the end of a psalm, the mechanism gave a click and the congregation were then regaled with a comic song entitled "Little Drops of Brandy", after which there was another click, and then "Go to the Devil and Wash Yourself". An even worse disaster occurred at Wannock, Sussex. Their clockwork barrel-organ could not be stopped, so they carried it outside into the graveyard and threw it into an open grave, where it is reputed to have played "All People that on Earth Below". The full story is told in the book "Barrel Organ" by Arthur W.J.G.Ord-Hume.

Most barrel-organs were turned manually with a handle, which did not exactly require a Doctorate in Music, but did need a certain amount of skill, apart from choosing the correct tunes from the barrel. The speed of turning the handle of course determined the pace of the singing, with the important reservation that if the player turned too slowly, the bellows did not give enough wind, and a sound like an expiring elephant ensued. Really expensive barrel-organs had two handles to overcome this problem.

Even musicians like Mozart and Handel (rather appropriately) composed tunes for the barrel-organ.

To a musical historian, the most exciting thing about barrel organs is that the person who pinned the barrels made the notes sound as they were actually sung and played at the time, and not as the tunes were written in the tune books. Long before the days of the gramophone, we actually have a "record" of the sounds they made. When we give our lecture-recitals, my friends play "Glory to Thee My God this Night" first as is appears in "Hymns Ancient and Modern", and then as it is pinned on the old barrel organ at Shelland in Suffolk. The latter version is full of lovely twiddly-bits, and most of the listeners prefer it to the modern stately version. Although I have never pinned a barrel organ, I did pin a barrel piano for St. Austell Rotary Club, which has raised many thousands of pounds for old peoples' comforts each Christmas. I had to transcribe the tunes already on the old barrel, write the new tunes to fit, mark out a new barrel, and make and insert 10,000 headless nails. It took me a year.

Barrel-organs were beautiful examples of engineering, and when an organist became available, the church would often have its barrel-organ converted to a "finger-organ", so called to distinguish it from a barrel-organ. Nobody calls them finger-organs today of course; we should just call them ordinary organs. As explained above, a barrel-organ seldom had a complete set of pipes, so if the player wanted to play every note on the keyboard, extra pipes had to be added.

We have found records of eight barrel-organs in Cornwall between 1820 and 1859. These were at Camborne, Carleen chapel, Gulval, Kenwyn, Madron, Redruth, St. Ives, and St. Austell. Canon MacDermott also mentions that there was an "automatic reed organ" at Probus. Langwill and Boston in their "Church and Chamber Barrel-Organs" tell us that the Camborne instrument had a drum and triangle, and the St. Ives instrument was bought in 1831 for £150, and restored by Mr Dixon Nance, Cumberland. It has a tune-list for one sacred and two secular barrels, but only one secular barrel survives. It has four stops plus a drum and triangle, and is now in the St. Ives museum (no, not the Tate). It is likely that there were a great many more which were not recorded. Eventually of course nearly every church and chapel acquired a proper organ, but at that point we lose interest from the gallery minstrel point of view. In 1831 Tregony church paid 7½d for "charcoal for organ". Perhaps it had got indigestion or flatulence?

REED ORGANS

As a cheaper alternative to the barrel-organ, a reed organ was often purchased, and we found records of 31 of these in Cornwall between 1842 and 1903. Indeed many of them still exist, and there is a modern reed organ in Old Town Church, St. Mary's, Isles of Scilly. Although they are both reed organs, strictly speaking the harmonium is not the same as the much more common American organ. The harmonium blows air through its reeds, while the American organ sucks. The harmonium has an expression stop which disconnects the air reservoir and air passes directly from the foot pedals to the reed chamber, the volume of tone being completely under the control of an experienced player. Rossini wrote an important part for the harmonium in his "Petite Messe Solonnelle" (1863). Whether church organists aspired to these musical heights is very doubtful.

I always thought I knew how to spell "harmonium", at least in the singular, but I began to have doubts when I read the church records for Pillaton. In 1891 they had a "Hormanium"; in 1892 it was a "Harmineil", and in 1893 it was a "Harminium".

The American organ does not have the same expression facility, but has a much softer and less strident tone. Some had magnificent casework, and even imitation pipes, like the instrument in Tregaminion church.

These organs all had what are known as "free" reeds. This does not mean they cost nothing, but that the reeds are free to vibrate on their own without being attached to a pipe, as in the reed stops of an ordinary organ. All sorts of variations on the basic ideas were made, for example the Seraphine by John Green of London, and the Aelophone by Day and Munch of London. Most of the "harmoniums" (or should I say "harmonia"?) we found in the records were probably American organs, but at Sheviock church there is still a very interesting "Aeolophon" by John F.Myers Patentor & Manufacturer, 83 Charlotte Street, Fitzroy Square, London. It was sold by C.F.Hocking of Fore Street, Devonport. A press report of July 1850 refers to it as a Seraphine, and records with pride the sad demise of the gallery minstrels, and their replacement by a proper choir with proper music.

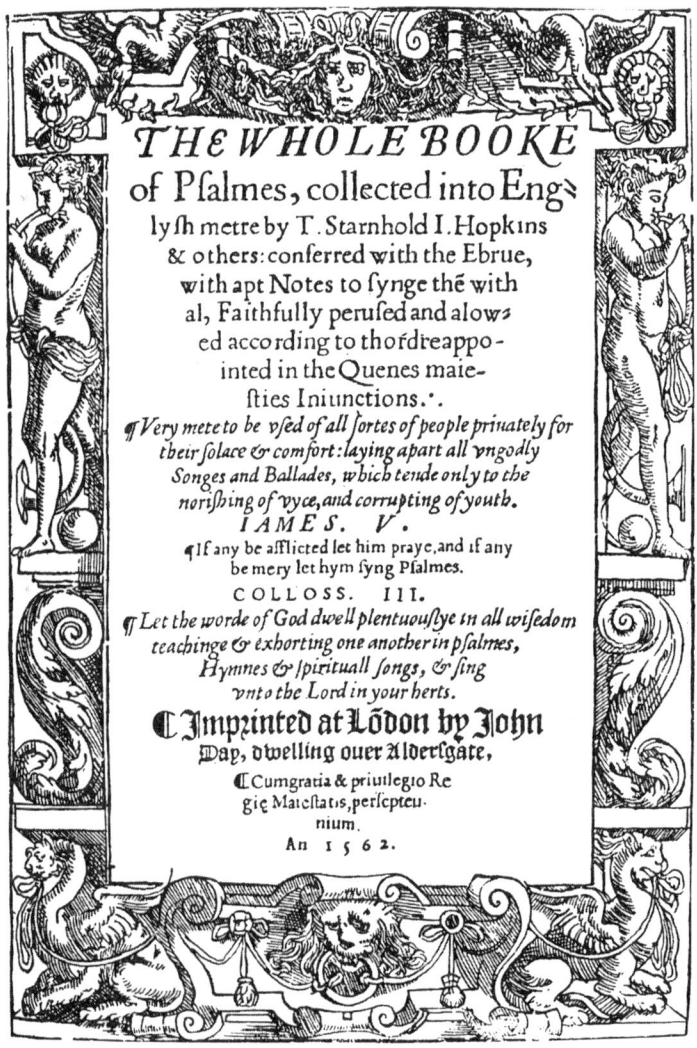

THE WHOLE BOOKE

of Psalmes, collected into Eng-
lysh metre by T. Starnhold I. Hopkins
& others: conferred with the Ebrue,
with apt Notes to synge thē with
al, Faithfully perused and alow-
ed according to thordre appointed in the Quenes maie-
sties Iniunctions.

¶ Very mete to be vsed of all sortes of people priuately for
their solace & comfort: laying apart all vngodly
Songes and Ballades, which tende only to the
norishing of vyce, and corrupting of youth.

IAMES. V.

¶ If any be afflicted let him praye, and if any
be mery let hym syng Psalmes.

COLLOSS. III.

¶ Let the worde of God dwell plentuouslye in all wisedom
teachinge & exhorting one another in psalmes,
Hymnes & spirituall songs, & sing
vnto the Lord in your herts.

¶ Imprinted at Lōdon by John
Day, dwelling ouer Aldersgate,

¶ Cum gratia & priuilegio Re
gię Maiestatis, persepteu-
nium.

An 1 5 6 2.

"Old Version" Sternhold & Hopkins, 1562.

CHAPTER FOUR

THE MUSIC

Hymn books are of course a fairly recent idea, but singing has always been part of the life of the Christian church. In ancient times "plain-song" was chanted (early church music with no harmony, and no rhythm other than that of the words), and some of this music was so effective that it is still sung in our churches today. An example is "Come Holy Ghost, our souls inspire" (Veni Creator Spiritus) which is often sung to the Proper Sarum Melody, dating from the ninth century. The history of music in our churches has been well researched by better scholars than I, and the reader is referred to the many excellent books in the appendix.

With the dawn of the Reformation the custom of congregational singing was revived, with English words instead of Latin. The psalms were rewritten in verse or metrical form, to enable them to be sung to music. These metrical psalms were not an official part of the prayer-book service, but were fitted in, in places where the service would not be disturbed. An injunction of Queen Elizabeth I said: "In the beginning or the end of Common Prayer there may be sung an hymn or suchlike song to the praise of Almighty God in the best sort of melody or music that may be conveniently devised, having respect that the sense of the hymn may be understood and perceived."

METRICAL PSALMS.

In 1549 Thomas Sternhold, Groom of the Robes to Henry VIII, translated and published 51 psalms. Sternhold did have a Cornish connection, because he bought Bodmin Priory on the Dissolution of the Monasteries. In 1562, 58 other psalms by John Hopkins and others were added. The book was published complete with music by John Day, and was known as "Day's Psalter", or more usually, simply as "Sternhold and Hopkins". This collection was immensely popular, and about 600 editions were produced. It became known eventually as the "Old Version". It should be noted that both Sternhold and Hopkins were laymen, and their efforts to versify the psalms outlived those of many clever clerics. No doubt the simple direct English, and the jingly rhymes, appealed to ordinary people, but not all of it was good poetry. How about Psalm 74, verse 12?

> *"Why doost withdraw Thy hand aback,*
> *And hide it in Thy lappe,*
> *O pluck it out and be not slack*
> *To give Thy foes a rappe."*

It was customary to print the metrical psalms at the back of the Book of Common Prayer, and I have one dated 1768 which contains Sternhold and Hopkin's version, but by then the poetry had been improved as follows:

"Why dost thou thy right hand withdraw
from us so long away?
Out of thy bosom pluck it forth
with speed thy foes to flay."

Tate and Brady published the "New Version" in 1696, which ran to about 130 editions, but some of the "Old Version" favourites stuck, the most famous of which was number 100, "All people that on earth do dwell", still known as the "Old Hundredth" today. "Tate and Brady" was still included in prayer books in 1857.

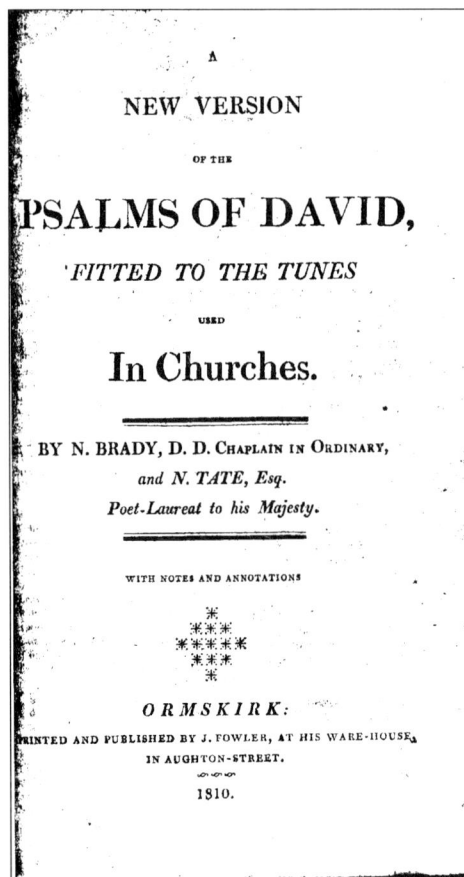

A

NEW VERSION

OF THE

PSALMS OF DAVID,

FITTED TO THE TUNES

USED

In Churches.

BY N. BRADY, D. D. Chaplain in Ordinary,
and N. TATE, Esq.
Poet-Laureat to his Majesty.

WITH NOTES AND ANNOTATIONS

ORMSKIRK:

PRINTED AND PUBLISHED BY J. FOWLER, AT HIS WARE-HOUSE,
IN AUGHTON-STREET.

1810.

The Cornish Catholic gentleman John Trevelyan referred to the metrical psalms as "Geneva Jigs". He was comparing them to what he regarded as pop church music from the protestants on the continent.

It is easy to laugh at the efforts of these pioneers, but their words caught the popular imagination, and in days when many could not read, the words were easy to remember and learn by heart. The Liskeard violin player John Welsh (c1840) could quote nearly all the metrical psalms from memory. However bad it may seem to us, this poetry brought the psalms to the homes of millions of churchgoers. Which poet of today will be remembered in 400 years time?

Between 1660 and 1860 hundreds of psalmodies

From "Psalmody improved" by Gresham c1780.

and hymn-books were published in England, many of them produced for a particular parish. As usually happens in life, some were good, some were bad, and some were awful.

In the last category we must put William Cole's setting of psalm XLI: "Blest is the Man whose Bowels move, And melt with Pity to the Poor, Whose Soul by sympathising Love, Feels what his Fellow Saints endure".

It is by no means easy to make the words of a psalm fit a tune. As a successful example we could quote this sentence from the Authorised version of the Bible: "Make a joyful noise unto the Lord, all ye lands, serve the Lord with gladness, come before his presence with singing". This appeared in the metrical version as: "All people that on earth do dwell, sing to the Lord with cheerful voice".

Not all arrangements were as successful as this. In the Dunstable psalm book, one goes:

> *"Of His great lib*
> *Of His great lib*
> *Of His great liberality".*

Another book has:
> *"Oh catch the flee*
> *Oh catch the flee*
> *Oh catch the fleeting hour".*

Then there was:
> *"Get me a man*
> *Get me a man*
> *Get me a mansion in the sky".*

And how about:
"Oh stir this stew
Oh stir this stew
Oh stir this stupid heart of mine".

My favourite is:
"Oh take thy morning pill
Oh take thy morning pill
Oh take thy mourning pilgrim home".

The worst disasters occurred when parts of the stanzas had to be repeated to fill up the tune. This is still common practice today, as in "O come all ye faithful" for example, but mercifully we try to avoid splitting words in half.

THE
WHOLE BOOK
OF
PSALMS:

WITH THE
Ufual *HYMNS* and Spiritual *SONGS*,
TOGETHER
With all the *Ancient* and *Proper* TUNES fung
in *Churches*, with fome of *Later Ufe*.

Compofed in THREE PARTS,
CANTUS, MEDIUS, & BASSUS:
In a more Plain and Ufeful Method than hath
been formerly Publifhed.

By JOHN PLAYFORD.

The Fourth Edition, Corrected and Amended.

PSAL. xlvii. Verf. 7.
God is King of all the Earth, fing ye Praifes with Underftanding.
EPHES. v. Verf. 19.
Speaking to your felves in Pfalms and Hymns, and Spiritual Songs, finging and making melody in your hearts unto the Lord.

LONDON,
Printed by J. Heptinftall, for the Company of STATIONERS: And are to be fold by Samuel Sprint at the Bell in Little-Britain; and Henry Playford at his Shop in the Temple-Change, Fleet-ftreet; and at his Houfe in Arundel-ftreet in the Strand, 1698.

"The Musickers" published in 1666 has a chapter on "Parochial Musick". It says: "The greatest blessing to lovers of music in a parish church, is to have an organ in it sufficiently powerful to render the voices of the clerk, and of those who join in his outcry, wholly inaudible".

Isaac Watts produced some of the better publications with his "Hymns and Spiritual Songs" of 1707, and his "Psalms of David" of 1719. Many of his hymns are still sung today, such as "When I survey the wondrous cross", and "Jesus shall reign where'er the sun". It should be emphasised that he wrote the words, not the tunes. Today certain tunes tend to be associated in our minds with certain words, but years ago any tune with the right metre might be sung to any set of words. The singers sometimes did not get this right either, as in one Methodist chapel in Cornwall when the hymn was in "common" metre (alternating 8 and 6 syllable lines), and some of the congregation were singing in "long" metre (all lines of 8 syllables). They did not discover their mistake until they reached the end, when one worthy remarked "A don't come in 'xactly, do 'a? But never mind, we can all'us double 'un arver a bit when the words waan't hold out" ("A Corner of Old Cornwall" by Mrs Bonham).

It was surprising how many sets of words could be sung to very few tunes. Rollo Woods, the historian and expert on West Gallery music, tells us of a Dorset band which played only two tunes, "thik" and "t'other". Despite this apparently serious shortcoming, Rollo tells us that it could have accompanied 96 psalms from the New Version, or 123 from the Old Version with just one common metre tune. Mr Woods is an excellent speaker, and during one of his lectures he told us about a poem he had found in one of his hymn books:

> "Steal not this book, for it is wrong,
> So put it down and go along,
> For when you die, the Lord may say,
> Where is that book you stole away?"

In the days when many were unable to read or write, and few had the money to buy books even if they could, the parish clerk used to introduce the metrical psalms, and then "line out" the words a line at a time, for the congregation to sing after him. As if this was not tedious enough, the musicians would often play an "interlude" between each verse, and even sometimes between each line. The 78th Psalm performed in this way and followed by a two-hour sermon must have given the congregation a pretty good idea of eternity.

Sometimes the interludes were totally inappropriate for their tune, and indeed we have found one in 3/4 time for a hymn in 4/4 time. Gresham published his "Psalmody Improved" in 1797 and it contains an unbelievably bad arrangement of the "Old Hundredth". My friends and I play it at our lecture-recitals, including its horrible interlude, but I am sure our audiences think we are making it up. I am afraid Gresham's "Psalmody Improved" had improved it for the worse.

Waltz or 3/4 time was very popular with the old musicians, and Canon MacDermott tells us that of 840 tunes published between 1789 and 1816, 46% were in 3/4 time. This compares with about 5% in 1861. Hymns were often chosen for their good tunes rather than being appropriate for the occasion, as when "Onward Christian soldiers, marching as to war" was sung after a wedding.

At Whitstone church in the 1860s the leader of the singing announced in his loud local brogue: "Let us zing to the praze and glory o'God, zaame sixty-two, Handel, altered a bit"! (press cutting, The Post & Weekly News).

Until the middle of the nineteenth century, the melodies of church tunes were sung by the tenor voices, not by the trebles as at the present time. This seems to be a survival from the days of plainsong, when the tenors sang the tunes when plainsong came to be written in four parts.

Although there were hundreds of printed music-books available, their cost was beyond the means of the average parishioner, so the musicians used to copy out their parts by hand, selecting of course the tunes which were popular in that particular church. These manuscript books were often minor works of art, with copperplate handwriting, and beautifully formed notes (even though the spelling might be somewhat wayward, and the harmony not to be found in any textbook).

HYMNS ANCIENT AND MODERN.

Whit Monday, 20th May, 1861, turned out to be a fateful day for church music. On that day the first edition of "Hymns Ancient and Modern" appeared. It was an enormous success, ran to over six editions with many supplements, and is still in use today. Sadly for historians, it rendered obsolete nearly all of the early psalmodies and hymn-books, especially the manuscript books so patiently copied out by hand, so that most of them probably finished up on the fire.

"Hymns Ancient and Modern" was of course a national publication, but it contained many hymns of Cornish provenance, and the work of the following Cornishmen:

E.A.Dayman was born in Padstow, and became a Fellow of Oxford, and Prebendary of Salisbury Cathedral. He was one of the editors of the "Sarum Hymnal", 1868, and wrote many translations and original hymns, including "O Lord be with us when we sail upon the lonely deep".

Thomas Haweis, despite a rather un-Cornish name, was born in Truro, where he studied medicine before taking Holy Orders. He went to Oxford, and in 1757 was appointed to a curacy there. He wrote the words to "O Thou, from whom all goodness flows", and the tune called "Richmond", or "Haweis", or "Spa Fields Chapel".

Most Cornishmen have heard of Robert Stephen Hawker, who became the vicar of Morwenstow. He was born just over the border, in Plymouth, and was educated at Oxford. He wrote "Sing to the Lord the children's hymn". It first appeared in his "Poetical Works", 1879, headed "The Song of the school, St. Mark's, Morwenstow" and dated 1840.

F.W.Newman was born in Falmouth, and became vicar of St. George's, Truro in 1889. He wrote "Jesus Lord of our salvation" for the dedication festival of St. George's.

Edward Osler was also born in Falmouth in 1798 of non-conformist parents. He joined the Church of England and studied medicine at Falmouth and Guy's hospital. He went to live in Truro in 1841, and edited the "Royal Cornwall Gazette". He contributed fifty hymns to the "Mitre Hymn Book", and wrote "O God unseen but ever near".

G.R.Prynne was born in West Looe, and went to Catherine's college, Cambridge. He became vicar of St. Peter's, Plymouth, in 1848. He wrote "Jesu, meek and gentle".

M.J.Monk (not the famous W.H.Monk who wrote the tune for "Abide with me"), was organist at Truro Cathedral. He wrote the tune "Give light".

W.Sloane-Evans went to Trinity College, Cambridge, and was vicar of Egloskerry until 1896. He wrote the tune "Clarion".

Mention should also be made of Sabine Baring-Gould, who became rector of Lew Trenchard in Devon. Although not Cornish, he wrote at length about west country matters, including "Old Country Life", with a charming account of "The Village Musician". By good luck I acquired from a junk shop one of his personal hymn books, "350 Hymn Tunes" by Harrison, published in London in 1888. It originally cost 3s 6d, but I only paid 1s 0d for it (5p!). It contains Baring-Gould's hymn "My Lord in glory reigning, upon the glassy sea".

"Hymns Ancient and Modern" has contained many tunes with Cornish titles, which may have had some Cornish connection, including "Gwennap", "St. Clement", "St. Just" and "Truro". Methodist hymn-books contained many more, including "St. Merryn", "Marazion", "Penzance", "Sennen Cove", "Cornwall", "Saltash", and "St. Enodoc".

CORNISH PRINTED MUSIC.

Cornwall has always been a stronghold of Methodism, and "Hymns Ancient and Modern" was rarely used in the chapels. John Wesley wrote a "Collection of Psalms and Hymns" in 1737, and had them printed in Charlestown (no, not Charlestown, Cornwall, but Charlestown, Georgia, USA). In 1738, after his return to England, John Wesley published another book with the same title, drawing freely from Isaac Watts and the "New Version". "Hymns and Sacred Poems" was published by John and Charles Wesley in 1739, followed by many more publications in their lifetimes. The Methodist Conference took over, and has been producing "Methodist Hymn-Books" to the present day.

DAVIDS HARP

Consisting of about **Three Hundred Tunes** *adapted to*

M.R WESLEYS *Selection of* HYMNS

One Hundred, of which Tunes are Originals Composed expresly

for this WORK by

Edward Miller Doctor in Music & his Son W. E. Miller

with an **Appendix** *Containing* **Pieces** for the

PRACTICE OF SOCIETIES OF SINGERS

Also Adapted for domestic use at the **PianoForte** *on a Sunday Evening*

Price 10.s 6.d

London — Printed for R.Lomas, at the New Chapel, City Road, & may had at Broderip
Wilkinson in the Haymarket, or of any Music or Bookseller in the Kingdom

A version of Wesley's Hymns.

The "precentor" of a cathedral is the person in charge of the song (literally "first singer") and the term goes back to the fourth century.   In 1895 the precentor of Truro cathedral sent out a questionnaire to all incumbents in the diocese of Truro, and asked them which hymn-books they were using. 222 replics were received. The results show clearly the outstanding success of "Hymns Ancient and Modern" in the Church of England:

"Church Hymns" (SPCK).................*3.6%*

"Hymns Ancient & Modern" *94.1%*

"Hymnal Companion"..................*1.8%*

Others...*0.5%*

We have searched for years and years to try to find some of these "others". Very few hymn books seem to have been published in Cornwall, or exclusively for Cornish churches. Whenever I visit a second-hand bookshop I ask if they have any old hymnbooks. The result is usually a few battered copies of "Hymns Ancient & Modern", but in the Arcade in Falmouth I was thrilled to find "The Cornubian Tune Book", by Richard Jones of Penzance. It was published by William Cornish, The Library, Penzance, in 1870, and contains 134 original tunes composed by the author, together with "Sanctuses" and "Glorias". The words are taken from "Hymns Ancient & Modern", Isaac Watts's hymns, Lady Huntingdon's Hymns, Wesley's Hymns, and others. The tunes are lovely, despite the composer's modest preface, which says that he is a self-taught man, and one who cannot play a single chord. His tune titles are a mixture of biblical names, personal names, and place names, together with a few miscellaneous names such as Glow-worm and Light Brigade.

Although not specifically Cornish, "The Bristol Tune Book" is fairly close to home, and contains many hymns with Cornish titles. The first edition was published in 1863, containing about 100 varieties of metre, and this was increased to nearly 200 by the issue of the second series in 1876. I have two versions of the third series, published in Bristol in 1891, and containing Lostwithiel, St. Austell, St. Feock, St. Keverne, St. Mabyn, and also St. Agnes and St. Columb, who may or may not be Cornish. We have performed Lostwithiel and St. Austell at our concerts, but I am afraid neither the tunes nor the words sound very edifying today. St. Feock, by Arthur H.Brown (who also wrote St. Austell), is set to a beautiful chant "Oh! for the peace that floweth as a river, Making life's desert places bloom and smile".

One or two Cornish hymns have been published in recent times, including "The Constantine Funeral Hymn" printed in the church guide by Mr. and Mrs. Fraser Harris in 1975. In 1946 J.Kitto Roberts in his "Mevagissey Independents" published the hymn "Furse". "This tune, composed by Precentor Furse, a member of the "Old Orchestra", rang out over Mevagissey, more than a hundred years ago". In the summer of 1993 the West Gallery Music Association published the Cornish hymn "Calynack" which will be mentioned again later on.

It has been claimed that Samuel Furley, a Calvinist minister, produced a hymn book at Roche in the 18th century, but we have never been able to verify this.

Ralph Dunstan was born in Carnon Downs in 1857, the son of William Dunstan the village carpenter. He joined Carnon Downs choir at the age of 12, and learned to play the piccolo, flute, euphonium, bassoon, and clarinet. We do not know for certain if he played in the chapel band, but it seems highly likely, because we know the chapel had a "bassoon and other wind instruments" in 1837, and did not have a harmonium until 1896. In 1877, at the age of 20, he went to London and entered Westminster Training College to train as a schoolmaster. In 1879 he completed his course with distinction, and went on to become a doctor of music. He became famous nationally for his liturgical music. He was also passionately interested in preserving old Cornish music, and in 1929 he compiled "The Cornish Song Book", under the patronage of the Royal Institution of Cornwall, the London Cornish Association, the Federation of Old Cornwall Societies, and the Cornish Gorsedd. It contains four Cornish funeral hymns, and of them Mr Dunstan says:

"From a manuscript book, yellow and tattered, which is at least a century old. The only instrument I ever heard at a funeral was the flute (sometimes two or three); it is perhaps a coincidence that Handel's "Dead March" opens with two flutes playing in thirds (singing in thirds is a very old Cornish custom)".

The tunes of the four hymns are "Sarah" by W.Arnold c.1800; "Chelsea"; "Cope", and "Hanover". He also produced "Cornish Dialect and Folk Songs", a "Book of Carols", and "One Hundred Methodist Tunes". He retired to Perranporth, where he died in 1935.

Of course, Cornish Christmas carols are well known, and a great many have been preserved for us in print. "The Cornish Song Book" mentioned above contains 53. There are many more in "Cornish Carols" published by Browsers Books, Falmouth; in "Carols for Cornwall" by Kenneth Polmear, in "Old Cornish Carols" by Leese, in "The Truro Carol Book" by Stubbs and Noble,and in the Truran publications "Twelve Cornish Carols" by Thomas Merritt, and "Canow Kernow" by Inglis Gundry. These carols and many others have been well researched by Cornish scholars, and are still performed each year, particularly in the Illogan area (Thomas Merritt's home town). One Cornish carol achieved national fame – it is in the Oxford Carol Book – the St. Day Carol, "Now the holly bears a berry as white as the milk". The composer is not known, but the tune seems to have originated near Gwennap in the late 18th century.

CORNISH MANUSCRIPT MUSIC.

We have been more fortunate in our search for Cornish manuscript music.

The tune book of Hannibal Lugg Lyne of St. Mawgan in Meneage, circa 1840, was preserved by the Cornish Methodist Historical Association, and is now in the care of the County Record Office, Truro (Their reference X 540/63). It contains 163 tunes, mostly with no words, but there are words to "Sovereign" and "Dismissal". A complete list of the contents is given in appendix 2. As will be seen, many of the tunes are known nationally, such as the Old Hundredth, New Sabbath, and Miles Lane. However, there are many which are of great interest to Cornish scholars.

Those with a likely Cornish connection are as follows:

> *St. Austle*
> *Belvedere or West Cornwall*
> *St. Austell new*
> *Chasewater*
> *Endellion*
> *Saint Clements*
> *Helston*
> *Calynack*
> *Bridgewater by Thomas Trethewey*
> *Falmouth*
> *Mawgan Chapel*

Neither of the St. Austells are the same as the tune in the Bristol Tune Book. Calynack has a great personal interest, because Kelynack was my wife's maiden name. The same name appears in the Domesday Book, spelt Chelenoch. The Cornish language is notorious for spelling variants, but the word means "holly grove", and there is still a place of that name near Land's End. Calynack has a jolly tune in 2/2 time, more like a dance than a hymn. As with all the tunes, the melody was written in the tenor part. We have re-written it in the modern way with the sopranos carrying the tune, and it has now been published by the West Gallery Music Association in their Summer 1993 Newsletter. It is very satisfying to bring a dead tune to life again after 150 years! Of course we do not know what words were sung to it, but "Come ye thankful people come" will fit the tune. We like best the words by John or Charles Wesley: "Glory be to God on high, God in whom we live and die".

I am a member of the Cornish Music Guild (Cowethas Ylow Kernewek), and its Director of the Archive, Dr Richard McGrady, found for me two

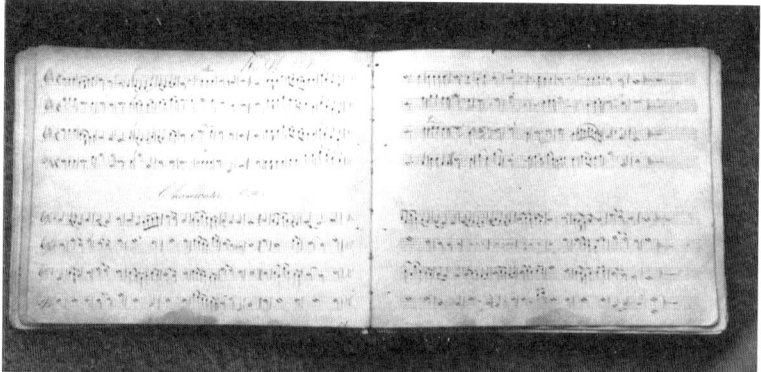

Tune book of Hannibal Lugg Lyne of St Mawgan in Meneage c1840.

Music books of Thomas Prisk, Carn Brea, Illogan c1838.

manuscript books which belonged to Thomas Prisk. They are half-bound in leather, now in rather poor condition with many leaves loose or missing. The large book has 117 surviving leaves of music with 8 staves per page in several hands: "Thomas Prisk Illog...."; "Thomas Prisk, Carne Brea, Cornwall"; "Thomas Prisk, Henry Libbey"; "His book and there is no doubt of its...............boys because he hath........". There is no date, but part-way through the book there is "Joseph Pryor his hand an pen dated march the 25th 1838".

The writers were labouring under difficulties, many "s"s being backwards, and one "f" upside down. There are some strange spellings: "Walsiugham", "Monmoth", "ST. Austll", (also St. Austle, which is the old spelling), "Jublee", "Manshans", "Aribea", and "Knaresbiragh". It is no wonder that some of the notes are queer too. Most tunes are in four parts, but where there is only one part, it is always the bass, so probably the book was used by a bass singer or instrumental player. One piece ("New York, Short Metre") has written on it "instrumental bass", so there was perhaps a cello or bassoon where the book was used. The hymns have no words, but one or two longer works have some words, e.g. "Vital Spark" (Pope's Ode). Some hymns occur more than once, for example "Tuckers", with just one note different. The writer must have forgotten he had already written it. I sometimes have the same problem!

Many tunes are well known from many sources, but these have a special Cornish interest:

> *? by S.Davey, Crowan.*
>
> *ST Austll.*
>
> *St. Austle by D.Tagg. (same tune)*
>
> *Falmouth.*
>
> *Trethewey.*
>
> *Trenorgie.*
>
> *Helston.*

The St Austles are the same as the St. Austle in Hannibal Lugg Lyne's book. Falmouth and Helston are also the same. Trethewey may be the composer to be mentioned presently.

The small book has 74 surviving leaves of music, 4 staves per page. It is in better condition than the large book, and appears to be all in the same hand. There is no date, and it begins: "Thomas Prisk's Music Book, Carne Brea, Illogan, Cornwall, England." One would have thought Cornwall might have been sufficient. As before , there are backward "s"s and odd spellings.

Most hymns are in four parts, but where there is only one part, it is always the bass. Some hymns are identical to those in the large book, e.g. Helston, and Falmouth (one note different). There are many hymns by A.Dunstan of Redruth. He could be a relation of Ralph Dunstan, but it is a common surname in the area. In addition, these have special Cornish interest:

> *Carn Brea.*
> *Falmouth.*
> *St. Leven.*
> *Redruth.*
> *Portreath.*
> *Helston.*

Towards the end, many tunes have "Trumpet Metre". "Josaih" and "Mercy" are marked for "instruments", and "voice".

Also in the Cornish Music Guild archive is a manuscript collection of "Old Cornish Carols" collected by Thomas M.Banfield of St. Ives (bardic name Cunteller Ylow). Amongst them are a few anthems and psalms, undated.

The contents of these books are shown in Appendix 3.

Miss Sybil Harris has been a leading figure in the music of the St. Austell area for a very long time. I first met her during the war, when I played the clarinet in the Tywardreath Youth Orchestra, and she was its accompa-

Trenoweth Chapel, Mabe.

In 1851 Thomas Reed took this serpent to America. He used to play it in Trenoweth Chapel, Mabe.

nist. For many years she has managed the St. Austell Music Festival. Her grandparents or great-grandparents, played the flute in Tregorrick Methodist Chapel before there was a harmonium. Miss Harris used to play the harmonium there, and later an American organ. She has kindly allowed me to copy the manuscript tune book which has been in her family for over 100 years. It contains St. Austell and St. Agnes, but most of the tunes are known nationally. The "St. Austell" is the same as "St.

71

Inside Trenoweth Chapel, Mabe.

Austell New" in Hannibal Lugg Lyne's book. The contents of Miss Harris's book are also shown in the Appendix 4.

I was highly delighted when a lady from Lostwithiel contacted me, to say that she had a manuscript tune book which belonged to her relative Thomas Trethewey (probably 1816-1870). I was even more delighted when she kindly allowed me to have a copy to study. The title page says: "A set of psalm, and hymn tunes, Composed by Thomas Trethewey, Breage". The book has 165 pages, containing 81 tunes, which all seem to be original compositions except the last one in the book: "Satisfaction (by Groom)". One tune, "Concord", has an extra bass line, and three tunes, "Priston", Brunswick", and "Bridegroom", have a section marked "ins" (instruments) and "voice", suggesting that the music may have been used with a band.

A lady from Truro wrote to me enclosing a photograph of the serpent her great-grandfather took with him to America in 1851. He used to play it (and possibly also a flute) in Trenoweth Chapel, Mabe. He also took with him his manuscript music book with its beautiful copper-plate handwriting. Fortunately two pages were later photocopied and returned to Cornwall. The title page says: "Thomas Reed, Trenoweth, Mabe. Thomas Reed his book...... the Feb 22, 1846". The other page is part of an anthem in four parts. The lady explained that the reason for the beautiful handwriting and elaborate lettering was that Thomas' grandmother wanted him to be a lawyer's clerk, and paid for him to go to school at Penryn until he was fifteen or sixteen. However, his father had no interest in him except behind the handles of a plough, so he had to work on his father's farms "Trelieves" and "Trenoweth" in Mabe parish.

We are still hoping that miracles will happen, and more of this manuscript music will come to light. If you discover any in your loft, in a car boot sale, or even around your fish and chips, do please let me know. The County Record Office in Truro would also be delighted to receive a copy for future researchers.

Waits of Beverley, Yorkshire (from a pillar in St. Mary's Church there).

CHAPTER FIVE

THE SOCIAL SCENE

Before the Commonwealth period the organ was the usual instrument to accompany the singing in cathedrals and large churches, as already explained. However, there are persistent but tantalisingly vague references to other instruments being used from the fifteenth to the early seventeenth century.

Town "waits" were originally watchmen, and in the days long before policemen, combined the duties of making music, waking people up in the morning, and keeping law and order. They played loud out-door instruments like shawms, primitive trumpets, sackbuts and even bagpipes. When Cardinal Wolsey visited St. Paul's Cathedral in 1527 he heard the "Te Deum" performed with the King's trumpets and shawms. Between 1500 and 1600 the waits became "tamed": they became indoor musicians, proud of the mastery of their instruments, and conscious of their higher social standing. They had to tame their instruments too, and make them more suitable for refined indoor music at social functions and banquets. They played cornetts and recorders as well as sackbuts, and later added viols, early stringed instruments. Inevitably , as they became more respectable, they were asked to play in church. The cornett covered the range of the higher vocal parts, and the sackbut covered the range of men's voices. This combination was used at Carlisle, Canterbury and Worcester in the early sixteenth century, and in 1575 the city waits of Norwich played in the cathedral. In time the Chapel Royal and several cathedrals were engaging their own bands.

The waits of Launceston are magnificently presented as granite carvings on the east end of the town's church of St. Mary Magdalene. There is even a Cornish bagpiper. The building of the church was started in 1511 and completed in 1524 but minor additions were made until 1538. The minstrels portrayed are well documented in the borough accounts. For 1467 there is an entry: "One quart of wine expended by the Mayor and his companions and the Mynstrelles in the vigil of the Blessed Mary Magdalene". It must have been quite an enjoyable vigil. The minstrels became famous in 1440 when Bishop Lacy granted a forty days' indulgence to all true penitents who gave money to support them. The granting of indulgences was a splendid scheme. The basic idea was that in return for money, the church would forgive you your sins for a specified period. Whether this could cover murder and robbery with violence, or just forgetting to say your prayers I do not know. The bishop is said to have granted this indulgence because of an incident which occurred during his visit to Launceston on 15th June 1440. He had come from

Okehampton, and was doubtless tired and weary after bumping along the rough roads in his carriage. As he came up the hill to Launceston he heard the strains of the Minstrels welcoming him from the hill-top, and is said to have exclaimed: "Holy Mother of Jesus, 'tis the angels singing". He named the place Angel Hill.

EARLY BANDS

There are several other very early references to town bands in Cornwall. For example in the borough accounts for St. Ives in 1576 we find: "Item pd the drommer at 2 musters ijs" (2 shillings). The able-bodied males of the parish were assembled for drill as a trained band, at regular intervals. In 1575 there is: "Itm payd to the pypers for there wages". By 1679 they seem to have got fed up with the drummer, for we find the item: "Expended on the Constables and Guard to put the drummer and his children out of Towne 8s 0d".

"Bodmin Riding" took place annually on St. Thomas' day, (7th July), said to be when the relics were returned to St. Petrock in 1177. The festivities lasted three days. Riding Ale was paraded round the town to the accompaniment of a drum and fife band playing the Riding Air, which is still played by Cornish folk bands today. The riding probably dates back to the sixteenth century, and has recently been revived.

In these early times there was a good incentive to go to church. At Penryn in 1694 "Every inhabitant found in the streets or playing games during the hours of divine service to be fined 8d". Perhaps this is the answer to the present crisis in church funding. If all those who were in the streets or playing games paid 8d, the church's problems would be solved.

It is difficult to say exactly when church bands started after the Commonwealth. Canon MacDermott suggests that they started in 1660, but quotes no evidence to support this. His excellent and valuable list of churches which had bands "between 1660 and 1860" contains no dates. Nicholas Temperley, that great authority on church music, considers that they were uncommon before 1770. His list of bands with dates covers the period 1780 to 1898. Our researches in Cornwall have found church instruments between 1785 (references to a clarinet and cello) and 1960 (clarinet and bassoon). We were excited to find in the church accounts for Lelant in 1737 "Pd Mr John Noall for Training of the Band and expenses 7s 0d". However, they bought a pitch pipe in 1760, so the "band" was probably a band of singers. An earlier entry for 1725 is "Paid expense when made Bargen with the singing master 15s 0d", so it is clear there was a singing-master there. In 1746 there is the entry "To a shoul and kilt for the sexon 2s 6d". Although nothing to do with gallery minstrels, it is nice to see a reference to a Cornish kilt! Later, in 1751 there is

"Paid for building the gallery and other work £9 0s 0d, Paid for part of the timber to build the loft £10 0s 0d". In 1752 there is "Paid Francis Richards for paint the loft 5s 0d". There are many entries for paying Samuel Hawes for attending the singing, and an amusing entry for 1758 "Paid Samuel Hawes for attendance an keeping fourth the singing 7s 0d". One wonders who was first, second and third.

The Madron church guide says "The rood screen was taken down in 1750 to make room for the orchestra". Such an early date for an orchestra is most unlikely.

Tracing early minstrel dates is made more difficult because keepers of church records often did not distinguish between singers and band. For example at Antony: "New violin for the singers £3 3s 0d"; at Camborne "The choir included many musical instruments". It was agreed at a special vestry meeting in Poundstock in 1847 that "the choir shall be paid for the strings which they find for their instruments". Otterham in 1824 bought "strings for the choir".

The legal basis of church music is complicated, to say the least. The Book of Common Prayer was abolished in 1645, and Cromwell made metrical psalms legal for the first time in history. The singing of hymns in the Church of England service has never been officially legalised, and until the end of the eighteenth century it was generally regarded as illegal. In 1820 proceedings were actually taken against a clergyman for introducing hymns into his service. However, the court decided not to prosecute. After this test case, hymns became increasingly popular.

INSIDE OUR CHURCHES

It is hard to imagine the scene at a church service at the end of the eighteenth century, the more so because our church interiors have been so drastically "improved". Most country churches would have had box pews. The only examples I know in Cornwall are the few still surviving at Launcells, but Veryan church had them until 1940. There are splendid examples at Minstead in Hampshire, Whitby in Yorkshire, and many other places in England. It is difficult to appreciate today that not all the congregation would be facing the altar. There were seats all round the inside of some box-pews, and many occupants would have their backs to the altar or the clergyman. The high sides and wooden doors were very effective at keeping out the draught, but also hid from the world any goings-on low down in the pew.

There was often a "three-tier" pulpit: the lower section being used by the parish clerk, the middle section by the parson for taking the service, and the upper section by the parson for delivering his sermon. To ensure the sermon was not too short, an hour glass was usually provided. There

Box pews in Launcells Church.

Box-pews and gallery, Zennor Church (before restoration).

are examples to be seen in Cornwall in the Trewint Wesley museum, and in the Launceston museum, where there is also a flute from North Tamerton. For my lecture-recitals I had a replica hour-glass made by a friendly glass-blower, set in a wooden frame made by my daughter. I searched everywhere for a suitable source of fine sand, and at last found some in the local pet shop. Apparently it is used for budgerigars. Unfortunately they also put chunks of oyster-shell in the sand. When I asked the shop assistant why they did this, she said "It's to stop people from using it to make hour-glasses".

There was usually a gallery at the west end of the church, where the singers and minstrels would perform. These were often fitted with curtains, as at Botus Fleming in 1810: "For new Curtains for the gallery and a new bag for the bass 9s 3d". In 1802 Illogan made "curtains for the gallery", as did Linkinhorne in 1827. Poundstock in 1798 had the entry in the accounts: "Pd Mr Watts for Sarge to make the curtings for the gallery 12s 2½". In 1826 they paid Mr Ash for "the skreen of the gallery £2 1s 8d". South Hill, near Callington, bought curtains for the gallery in 1800. In 1804 Launceston bought "Stuff for a schreen for the singers 5s 4d". St. Stephens by Saltash in 1804 "Pd Mr Smith for the Curtains & Rods for the Gallery" and also "Pd for Fringe for the curtain of the Gallery". In 1823 they were paying 9s 2d for "Drying the Gallery Curtains". I wonder how they got wet? St. Tudy in 1820 bought a gilded knob for the gallery, and in 1832 Week St. Mary paid John Hicks "for 4 knobs used about the screen in the gallery". In 1847 Talland paid for "drawers in gallery" (presumably not the kind you wear).

In Stratton in 1810 the vestry "inspected" the gallery (cost 3s 0d). We have never found such an entry in church accounts before, so this must have been quite an occasion. Shortly after this they bought 15 yards of "stuff" for the gallery. I wonder if this was for curtains, or seating, or to mute the sound somewhat. At Sheviock in 1818 they paid Thomas Stark "for making matting for singing seats".

Gallery expenditure always included "candles for the singers". All this conjures up a lovely picture of the musicians in their cosy gallery, where the public were not allowed, surrounded by their curtains, fringes and brass knobs, dimly lit by candle-light, drinking and smoking during the interminable sermons.

There are many accounts in England of the musicians putting their hats on the altar during the service. This seems rather irreverent to us today, but altars then were not respected in the same way. They had a better idea in Morwenstow in 1814, when they spent 2s 0d "for a pin to hang up the Hatts etc". In London the vicar of a West End church made the following startling announcement. "The special preachers during this solemn season of the year will be found hanging in the porch as you leave the church".

Dr Syntax preaching from a three tier pulpit. (Thought to be St. Breward church). c.1812.

3-Decker Pulpit in Minstead church, near Southampton.

Some pictures have come down to us of church interiors during this period. Canon MacDermott has three in his book, the best of which being a reproduction of "The Village Choir", a painting by Thomas Webster, R.A., which hangs in the Victoria and Albert Museum. Nicholas Temperley has some excellent pictures in his book "The Music of the English Church", especially a 1790 print by J.Wright "Sunday Matins in a Village Church". The slightly inebriated gallery minstrels are leaning dangerously over the edge of their gallery.

In the parish church of St. Breward on Bodmin Moor, there is a copy of a print of "Dr Syntax Preaching" by Thomas Rowlandson (1756-1827), showing the interior of St. Breward church in the early 19th century. There is a gallery in the west end. Although many features of the church are wildly inaccurate, the picture does perhaps give an impression of the atmosphere during a service of that period.

Amongst the Thomas Hardy papers in Dorset is a plan of the seating for singers and musicians in Stinsford church in 1835 (see p.4). Although no such plan is known for Cornwall, the arrangement was probably similar. (One of my more pedantic friends objects to my distinguishing between singers and musicians. I do apologise – the singers were doubtless musicians too).

Our Cornish records show that church and chapel bands here had from one to eight players. The largest bands were at Liskeard Greenbank chapel (8); and Madron, Liskeard, and St. Mawgan in Pydar churches which had 6. Inevitably our records miss out any instruments which were maintained by their owners. Bands of one seem intrinsically unlikely, unless the instrument is playing the bass part.

Inside the Methodist Museum, Trewint.

"The Village Choir" by Thomas Webster.

Sunday Matins in a village church in 1790.

PARISH CLERKS

Parish clerks in our churches go back at least to the 15th century, when they assisted the priest with the reading of psalms and responses. By the 18th century, they had a wide range of duties. They announced the metrical psalms, and read them out a line at a time for the congregation to sing; often led the singing, and sometimes led the band as well, or turned the handle of the barrel organ. They were very poorly paid, and often had little training or aptitude for their musical duties. They were also involved in keeping parochial death statistics: some were so poor that they supervised the death statistics at close quarters because they were also sextons. The parish clerk at Newlyn East seems to have been a builder; he built their gallery in 1823. By the end of the 19th century there were very few parish clerks left in England.

In the old days, when the parish clerk used to give out the church notices, there were many occasions for mirth. One clerk announced "The Archdeacon will attend on Wednesday next to swear at the church-wardens" One old Shropshire clerk announced on Easter Day "Last Friday was Good Friday, but we've forgotten un, so next Friday will be he".

I like the story of the parish clerk who fell asleep in a field. A sheep came up to him and made a loud "Baa!" Thinking it must be the end of a prayer, the clerk said "Amen".

There is an epitaph to a parish clerk in Scothorne, in Lincolnshire, to John Blackburne, who died in 1739:

> "Alas poor John
> Is dead and gone
> Who oft toll'd the bell
> And with a spade
> Dug many a grave,
> And said "Amen" as well".

In a typical church in Cornwall in the late 18th century, there would be a metrical psalm before the sermon. The parish clerk would announce it from his place at the bottom of the three-tier pulpit (for the benefit of anyone who had a book, and could read it), then walk back to the gallery to lead the singing. The clergyman would go into the vestry to change from his surplice into his black "Geneva gown" while the psalm was being sung, then return to climb the steps to the top deck of the pulpit to deliver his sermon. He took no part in the singing if he could possibly avoid it. He would return to the vestry during the singing of another metrical psalm.

COSTS OF PROVIDING THE MUSIC

It was far from clear whether the costs of providing the music could be charged to the parish. For example at Kettering, Northamptonshire in 1817 the vestry refused to re-imburse a churchwarden who had paid for organ repairs. In Cornwall there were frequent arguments about the payments to the musicians, though this probably reflected poor performance rather than any legal implications.

At East Looe in 1863 it was resolved "That the above accounts having been examined be allowed and passed with the understanding that no amount for singers be charged in future". All good strong stuff, except that by 1868 we read: "James Jeffery for Singing £2 0s 0d". In 1873 they bought a harmonium by subscriptions. We notice they did not try to buy it from church funds.

At Landulph in 1849 we have the entry: "It may however be fairly inferred from the entries in the Church Book that the Bequest was for the Maintenance of the Church to which it has been applied in aid of the church rate. Some payments appear of a peculiar nature for Teaching the Singing, for Instruments, Music Books, Treats to Singers, Dinners on account days, for Vermine caught which can hardly be termed "Repairs of the Church". There is also a query about "Wine to the parson" sometimes found. Perhaps they had a new young curate who did not know the ropes. Anyway in 1859 they bought a harmonium from church funds. This did not seem to do them much good, because there were repair bills every year until 1871, when they bought another one from Moon & Sons for £17 19s 6d.

At Forrabury, Boscastle in 1834 it was "unanimously resolved that the singers have been very neglectful and do not deserve the Singing Money and until they Better Deserve it we propose Leaving it in the hands of the Churchwarden until the Sense of the Parishioners can be obtained".

In 1849 Tywardreath paid Mr E.Rosevearne for teaching the singers £1 0s 0d, and a treat for the singers £2 0s 0d, but a vestry meeting on 4th April 1850 disallowed both of the above expenditures. What a swindle! And who finished up paying I wonder?

They were obviously worried at Lanteglos in 1851, but after debate, "It was resolved that payment to the singers for the last 20 years be continued".

The vestry meeting in Poughill in 1834 decided that "the two pounds now allowed to the singers shall be discontinued", but they paid it again in 1835. Either they had short memories, or perhaps a new council was elected. They obviously had a guilty conscience as far as music was concerned, because in 1843 they paid Mr Perry for violoncello strings, then wrote in the accounts "Not allowed". Perhaps he played lots of wrong notes.

It was not usual to pay the singers or the band directly, but to reward them with a feast, as has already been described. However, at Tywardreath in 1797 they paid "Clark's fees and blewing the hautboy (oboe) £2 10 0d". At Crantock in 1830 they paid Elias Carrwick for playing the bass viol, and paid 6 girls for singing 6s each. In 1836 they paid the female singers £1 2s 0d, and the men singers £1 13s 0d. There may have been more men, or perhaps they sang louder. The chapel in Penryn in 1829 paid its female singers 30s and its "man singers" 20s, but by 1833 the equal pay lobby had increased all singers' pay to £2 6s 6d.

CLOTHING

A good idea of the clothes worn by the minstrels and singers can be obtained from the pictures already mentioned. The country yokels would wear their Sunday best, but this might only be a cleaner-than-average smock. Canon MacDermott describes their smock-frocks, brown fustian knee-breeches and buskins. Fustian is a thick twilled cotton cloth with a short nap, and buskins are calf- or knee-high boots of cloth or leather (like the ones worn in the Middle Ages). He says that in Brightling church about 1820, the men wore yellow stockings with their buckskin breeches, and the ladies wore red cloaks. The girls in an old choir wore white straw poke-bonnets, trimmed with cambric, with pink and white print dresses and capes. H.Smith's 1859 etching of Mr Pennicott playing the clarinet shows him smartly dressed in a suit, with high wing-collar and cravat, and his top-hat on the window-ledge.

William Tuck tells us that before 1800 in Camborne, "The musical part of the church service was sung by men who used to wear leather breeches and buff gloves".

When members of the West Gallery Music Association performed for the BBC in their "Songs of Praise" programme in 1990, we all had to be very careful of our dress. Rollo Woods prepared a booklet advising us what to do. I wore a smock made for me by my wife, with my old gardening corduroy trousers cut down to make breeches with buttons on the sides, and long grey socks. We hunted everywhere for a red kerchief with white spots, to go round my neck, but in vain. Apparently it was no longer the fashion in 1990. I remember the gypsies used to carry their lunch in such kerchiefs when I was a boy. Finally we found a red spotted frock in a charity shop in Plymouth, and my wife cut it down to make a splendid kerchief. I told all my friends I had been to Plymouth to buy my wife a dress in the Oxfam shop. She was not amused. The final problem was my glasses, which were obviously 20th century. My friend Mr Watts, an antique dealer, solved this problem with a genuine antique pair with brass rims. They looked ideal from the outside in, but from the inside out there was a big problem. I could hardly see anything!

RIBBONS

In the Cornish records we have found several references to "ribbons for the singers". We know that ribbons were popular presents for young ladies in that period – for example "Oh dear, what can the matter be.........
He promised to buy me a bunch of blue ribbons to tie up my bonnie brown hair". I'm afraid modern young ladies would not be very impressed with blue ribbons as a present. However, I would love to know what they did with their ribbons, and where they wore them. The church gallery pictures show the ladies wearing ribbons around their bonnets, but how many yards would that take?

Lanreath bought 9 yards of ribbon at 6d per yard for their singers in 1791. They bought another 64 yards in 1793, 12½ yards in 1794, 7 yards in 1795, 9 yards in 1796, 9½ yards in 1797, and unspecified lengths in every year until 1805. Judging from the costs they must have bought about 146 yards altogether, enough to have completely clothed all the girls I would have thought.

St. Tudy has an entry for 1795: "Pd for 12 yds of Ribbonds for the Girls 6s 0d", and similar entries for 1798, 1800, 1804, and 1806. The payments then stop, and instead in 1809 we find: "Pd for Liquor for the singers £1 6s 9d". The singers seem to have grown up, and become more expensive in the process.

St. Neot in 1819 bought "ribbons for the treble singers 4s 6d".

It is strange that these were the only three churches where we found such entries in the accounts.

St Neot was not the only church to show special favour to the trebles. Liskeard in 1816 paid for "Trebles for Tea"; in 1817 had a "Trebles Tea Feast", and in 1819 and 1820 had a "Singers' Feast, Trebles' Tea".

DID CHURCH BANDS PLAY ELSEWHERE?

It has proved quite difficult to find positive evidence that the church gallery minstrels also played for social events in the towns and villages, although it seems pretty obvious that they must have done. There would not have been so much musical talent around that separate bands could be formed. Nicholas Temperley tells us: "In all parts of the country, however, the church musicians, particularly the instrumentalists, were figures of considerable standing in village life. One must not imagine that these musicians played only in the church. They were concerned with the

"Old Church Orchestra."

whole social and festive life of their village, and took their part in the dance, the harvest home, the Christmas carol, the flower show, the club feast". He also tells us that many bands played in both churches and chapels.

In "Life's Little Day", published early this century, Mrs Stirling tells the story of a church near Southampton. The orchestra consisted of three or four old men, who also played dance music at parties in the village. One Christmas the musicians were so tired out that they all fell asleep during the sermon. At the end the parson gave out the hymn, whereupon the leader of the orchestra woke with a horrified start, nudged his fellow musicians, and still half asleep all struck up "Sir Roger de Coverley". Up jumped the squire in his pew, turned round, and wrathfully waving the luckless musicians to silence, exclaimed, "For this insult to me, my family, and Almighty God you shall no longer play in this church. I will give an organ".

Inglis Gundry, the Cornish composer, tells us in his "Canow Kernow" (1982) of a "Peter B. who played a rogue's march in a meeting house by mistake". He presumably played in the local pub during the week.

In 1832 some members of the Launceston chapel choir were reprimanded by the trustees for attending the theatre with their instruments.

"The Village Orchestra" from a Kenwyn Church booklet, Truro.
clarionet, serpent, flute, bass viol, violin and bassoon

John Probert tells us of the band at St. Erth who played in church in the morning, and in chapel at night.

There was a church band at Morwenstow, which was made obsolete by the purchase of a harmonium, but the same players continued to play for local village events, and indeed the descendants of these players were still in the Morwenstow band in recent times. Cornwall is famous for its bands, and it is likely that many of its players are descended from the old church gallery minstrels.

No doubt the same musicians played for dancing round the Maypole on May Day, and it is delightful to see the event still taking place each year in the Isles of Scilly.

Every five years the John Knill celebrations take place in St. Ives. John Knill was born in Callington in 1733, and was a customs officer in St. Ives from 1762 until 1782, becoming Mayor in 1767. He had a great affection for St. Ives, and was determined to be remembered by its inhabitants "a little longer than the usual time of those (for) whom there is no ostensible memorial". He built a steeple-shaped mausoleum on the top of Worvas Hill, and set up a trust fund to provide for celebrations every five years. The trustees are the Mayor, Vicar, and Customs Officer for St. Ives at the time. For the celebrations the trustees choose a Master of Ceremonies; a fiddler; ten little girls who are the daughters of seamen, fishermen, or tinners; and two widows. After jollifications in the town, they all go to the mausoleum to sing the "Old Hundredth" after dancing around the monument. It is most interesting that the legacy includes "£5 for white ribbon for breast knots" – so that is what they used to do with their ribbons. The final irony was that John Knill was not buried in his mausoleum after all. It contains his empty sarcophagus. Because of problems with consecration, he was buried in England at Holborn, London, when he died in 1811.

No doubt the gallery musicians played at local feasts, which were celebrated in towns and villages in Cornwall since very early times. For example St. Austell had its feast day on Trinity Sunday and the three following days. St. Ives had its feast day on the nearest Sunday to 3rd February. Luxulyan feast day was the Sunday preceding the 24th June, and lasted until the Wednesday evening. Par had its feasts on 2nd February and 24th June, and Mevagissey feast started on St. Peter's Day, 29th June, and went on for a week.

When I was a boy at Carclaze Infants' School in the 1930's, Carclaze feast was celebrated every year. The afternoon was a holiday, and we were all given saffron buns and lemonade. We danced in the field across the road to the sound of a brass band – from Mount Charles I think.

STORIES OF THE GALLERY MINSTRELS

Delightful tales of the gallery minstrels in our churches are told by Thomas Hardy in his novel "Under the Greenwood Tree" (1872 and many subsequent editions); by Sir Arthur Quiller-Couch in "The Looe Diehards" from "Wandering Heath" (1895); by Charles Lee in "The City" – "The Portrait of a Cornish Musician"; and by the Rev Baring Gould in his "Old Country Life" (1890). These books should be available in Cornish libraries, and the reader is strongly recommended to enjoy them. I love browsing in second-hand bookshops, and we are fortunate in Cornwall in having so many. I usually make for the "Religion" section, but I am afraid the vast majority of books on religion, especially books of sermons, are rather beyond the limits of my patience to read. However, there is a marvellous book by J.A.Latrobe with the rather long-winded title: "The music of the Church considered in its various branches, congregational and choral". In a delightfully rambling style, it paints pictures of incompetence and disaster in our churches. Here are one or two examples:

"Singers and performers are preparing in the gallery to make their best display. At the appointed time they commence. The first specimen he has of his choir is perhaps ushered in by the clarinet, which, though rather a favourite in country churches, is the most hapless in untutored hands. This is commissioned to lead off, and after some dreadful hiccups on the part of the instrument, which is its infirmity when clumsily dealt with, and which chases the blood chill through the veins, the tune is completed, and the singing proceeds. Then the other instruments are introduced – "the flute, and the vile squeaking of the wry-necked fife", and it may be, breaking suddenly in with portentous thunder, after three or four notes spent in gathering up the long clambering instrument, some unlucky, deep-mouthed bassoon. It may readily be conceived, that these instruments by their united clamour, will lay a sufficient foundation of noise, upon which the singers may rear their superstructure. This they proceed to do with their whole breadth of lungs, each striving to surpass his neighbour in vociferation; till, exhausted with the exercise, they gradually cease, according to the tenure of their breath; the bassoon player, for the dignity of his instrument, commencing his last note rather later than the rest, and, by a peculiar motion of his shoulders, pumping out the whole power of his lungs in one prolonged and astounding roar. All sit down – a smile of self-congratulation playing about the lip, supposing that they have given their new parson a good idea of the manner in which they can anticipate the joys of heaven, as if "the air of paradise did fan the house, and angels officed all"".

Latrobe goes on to explain how the parson can bring some sort of dignity to this chaos:

"Then the instruments, badly sorted and worse played, might attract his notice. The bassoon must be dispensed with at all hazard; and if a violoncello can be introduced into its place, an important object is affected. The fife may be easily put down, and even though the clarinet should be suffered to remain with the flute, the evils arising from bad performance will be less perceived, when the tune is restored to its proper character".

Having finally got rid of the band, Latrobe turns his attention to the singers. We wondered earlier about the function of curtains in galleries. All is now made clear:

"The natural modesty of the female character requires, that in the performance of their sacred duties, "the singing women" should not be too prominently exposed to public gaze. Nothing is more beautiful and feminine than retiring modesty; if removed, there is no artifice that can compensate for the defect: the jewel has lost its polish. Not even a sacred employment may demand the sacrifice of that glory of the woman which is typified in her long hair. What can be more unpleasing, than to see a female with unabashed front, standing up in the presence of the full congregation, and with outstretched neck, screaming above the voices of the multitude, and the swell of the organ, like a seagull in a tempest! How much better, that the diffidence which so well becomes woman in private life, should accompany her to the great congregation; that where her services are needed, they may be afforded without violence to delicate feelings – the curtain screening her from unnecessary observation!"

THE WESLEYS

With these sorts of goings-on in the churches, it is perhaps not surprising that Wesley's preaching fell on fertile ground. John and Charles Wesley first visited Cornwall in 1743, and soon acquired a large following. Methodist chapels were built all over the county, often with very little money and a great deal of practical support by the congregation. Many of them started their life with a band of musicians before they could afford a harmonium or an organ. There were other non-conformist groups too, Baptists and Bible-Christians among them. I was always puzzled as a boy how they managed to build Christian chapels before the time of Christ. They all had "B.C.Chapel" above the door!

At Goonpiper chapel, Feock, built in 1867, they had an orchestra to lead the singing on Sundays. The preachers arrived on horseback, so a stable was an important part of the premises. Carnon Downs chapel was built about 1824, and ten years later a piece of land next to it was granted to a Mr Morton on condition that no public house or kiddleywink should be built on it. The chapel was lit by 80 candles (tallow dips). In 1837 there was a choir, and the singing was led by wind instruments – "Uncle Ebb could make that bassoon of his almost speak". They bought a harmonium in 1896. (from "Feock with Carnon Downs in the 19th century", University of Exeter, 1977).

Non-conformist chapel records are not as easily accessible as church records, but where they can be found, they shed an interesting light on chapel bands. At Sticker chapel in 1847: "The Bafs Vile Bought about this time to which the Trustees paid £2 towards is to be reckoned as belonging to Sticker Chapel; no individual shall have any claim". In 1841: "Borrowed of Jn Clarke sum to defray the expense of a new pulpit and new sleepers under the singing seat £8 0s 0d". By sleepers they meant timber reinforcements. In the Church of England the sleepers were usually on the seats. In 1856 they bought a harmonium, but surprisingly bought a flute at the same time: "Bought a Harmonium for the Chapple £23 0s 0d. Bought a Flute for the Chapple 15s 0d. Expenses going after it to Truro 1s 4d". See page 23 for an explanation of "going after".

At Charlestown Wesleyan chapel in 1835: "That the sum of 19s 6d shall be paid for a book in which the Singers may enter their music, which book shall be the Property of the Chapel and be marked with a bold letter on the outside the cover Charlestown Wesleyan Chapel". In 1841: "It is particularly requested that no Singer shall bring their child or Children into the seats. That what expense be attendant on the Base File shall be paid by the Trustees of the Chaple". Then in 1849: "Resolved that the Trustees do not object to the introduction of a Seraphine – provided the same can be purchased by subscription and become the property of the Trust".

John Probert has a treasure trove of lovely stories about Wesleyan chapels in his book "The Worship and Devotion of Cornish Methodism". Amongst them are these three:

Mr Lazarus Evans, who worked at St. Day brickworks early this century, had a good voice, and sang the anthems from memory. He could often be seen in the chapel choir with his anthem sheet upside down, because he could not read.

The congregation at Roscroggan chapel were singing the words "We shall sing more sweet more loud", and a passer-by commented "sweeter maybe, louder never!"

At Lanner Hill before the last war there was to be a service of song and the chapel was full. The steward came out and said "Sorry friends, we can't start. The organ is gone wrong and the chairman isn't arrived. I tell you friends we are in some stank".

John Wesley used to preach at our famous Gwennap Pit, and our little group, the "Old Church Gallery Minstrels", had the privilege of giving a lecture-recital there. As far as we know there is no record of musicians playing there in the past.

VISITS TO OTHER CHURCHES

Church singers and band were often invited to perform at other churches, and these visits are well documented in the records. For example: "Around 1860 men and boys of Mousehole choir set out from the village at midnight on Christmas Eve, and sang their way to Paul churchtown and other places nearby: Richard Barnes led the trebles with his violin, his father – George Barnes _ the basses with a bass-viol, James Harvey the tenors with a violin, and Mr Bond of Newlyn, the altos with a flute. Perhaps they travelled as far as Hellesveor choir which, in 1874, took their instruments, cornet, clarinet, ophicleide, etc and sang carols on a tour that lasted through the night" ("A History of Cornish Methodism" by Thomas Shaw).

The accounts for St. Clement's in 1816 have the entry: "Meat for the Gwennap Singers 15s 6d, for Liquor and Bread for the same £1 6s 5d". Similar entries can be found for 1774 when the Werrington singers visited Egloskerry; for 1781 when Paul visited Madron; for 1807 when Probus visited Kenwyn; for 1834 when St. Gennys visited Jacobstow; for 1835 when Sancreed visited Buryan; for 1866 when Altarnun visited St. Clether; and many, many more. Some churches made a habit of it: Lanreath church was visited by the singers from Pelynt, Lanteglos, Duloe, Lansallos, Liskeard, Morval, and St. Martins Looe (called "St. Martyn de Loo" in the old episcopal records).

These visits were clearly important social events, but it is not entirely clear what the resident singers did. Did they join in the singing with the visitors, or were they visiting another church themselves? No doubt these visits encouraged competition, as each group tried to become the best in the neighbourhood. At Long Ashton near Bristol the clerk noticed an unusual number of Bristolians present, and said "If any of you musical chaps be here from Bristol, come up in the gallery and give us a hand with the anthem".

There were also outings for the musicians. For example St. Minver church choir had an outing in 1896, costing 4s 3d. The accounts do not say where they went.

SINGING MASTERS

C hurch choirs employed singing-masters from an early date, and there is much information about them in the church records. Nicholas Temperley describes them as "self-taught musicians who provided and led the music of country churches c. 1680-1850". The earliest mention we have found in Cornwall is for 1698 in St. Ives, when they spent 2s 0d on Mr Morgan, the singing-master. Singing-masters were often itinerant, and covered several parishes. Students of Cornish will be amused to see a reference at Lelant in 1797 for "learning" the singers. In Cornish the word "dysky" means either to learn or to teach.

Our studies have found references to singing-masters in the records of forty-three churches, and one hundred and fifty-five are mentioned by name, covering the period from 1737 to 1858.

In a few parishes it appears that the teaching was shared between two persons, for example at Lewannick from 1828 to 1831: "Messrs Wearing and Bennet for attending the singing £2 0s 0d". There appear to have been two singing-masters for short periods at St. Dominic, Lawhitton, and Tywardreath. Some of them held office for a long time: Richard Frain (or Frayne) was choirmaster at Egloskerry from 1781 until 1811, followed by John Frain in 1813. At Lewannick in 1810 a payment was made to Robert Frein of Trewin. They seem to have been a musical family.

A village choir rehearsal in 1863.

At Trewen in 1797 was recorded: "To Mr Richard Frayne - teaching ten tunes at 5d each. This sounds a hard way of earning a living.

There were also visiting singing-masters. At Antony, near Torpoint, from 1801 until 1811, Mr Coombs was paid "23 nights instructing singers £5 15s 0d", then for the next two years his payment also included "board and hospitality". The following year this became "board of himself and horse".

Payments to singing-masters generally varied from about 5s 0d to £2 2s 0d a year, with a few instances of larger amounts; for example at North Tamerton in 1775 it was £5 5s 0d. Such figures can be converted to modern currency as follows:

> *5s 0d then is about £12 in 1996.*
>
> *£2 2s 0d then is about £100 in 1996.*
>
> *£5 5s 0d then is about £250 in 1996.*

No doubt the range indicated many things: the skill and qualifications of the singing-master; the available funds of the church; the enthusiasm of the church wardens and vicar for music. Sometimes, as at St. Antony, the singing-master had to provide strings and instrument repairs out of his salary. Quite frequently the singing-master was also the clerk, and played an instrument in the band himself.

The "singing-masters" at St. Agnes appear to have been Mrs Carne in 1819, and Miss Vawdery in 1872. In all the other records we have studied, they were men.

REPAIRS TO MUSIC AND INSTRUMENTS

There are several references in the church records to "pricking" the music. For example at Lanreath in 1793 "To Henry for Pricking the Singing Books 10s 0d", and at Kenwyn in 1788: "For Pricking Musick 5s 10d", "To Mr Brown for writing 70 pages of Musick 5s 10d", and in 1789: "Deduct Sam Brown pricking tunes twice 5s 10d". It seems clear from this last entry that writing and pricking the music meant the same thing. Early elaborate polyphonic music was originally called "pricksong", and in 1562 a copyist was paid for "Pricking 27 songs". It looks as though this ancient word was carried over to mean copying or arranging the notes of the music.

Music books, and of course musical instruments, required frequent repairs. For example at St. Clement's in 1808: "To Mr Winterbotham for repairing Music 7s 6d". At St. Gennys in 1807 the exasperation of the churchwarden can be sensed: "Strings for violin 5s 0d", "For string for violin more 1s 0d". St. Martin-by-Looe had a flute in 1820, but either it was in poor condition, or the player was rather heavy-handed. It needed repairing every year. In his excellent book "Music and Musicians in Early 19th Century Cornwall", Dr Richard MacGrady tells the story of the negro slave Joseph Emidy, who played the violin, and settled in Falmouth. We found in the accounts for Crantock for 1830: "Paid Thos. Emidy for Repairing Violoncello 10s 6d", and again in the St. Michael Penkevil accounts for 1838: "Paid to Thos. Emidy for repairing the Bass Vile £1". It is likely that Thomas came from the same family.

When major alterations to the church were needed, the Church of England required a "Faculty" to be approved by the Bishop. These were produced for galleries, and for installing organs. For example there were faculties at Pelynt in 1728 to erect a gallery, and at Poundstock in 1891 to remove the gallery.

Church vandalism is no new thing. St Eval in 1841 "Paid for Printing hand Bills offering a Reward for Breaking the Church Door open 6s 5d".

At St. Dominic in 1783 there was a curious entry in the accounts: "Pd for a sheet of Stampt Paper for a Bond for the singers 6s 1d". We do not know what this Bond was for.

FUNERALS

We cannot close this chapter without saying something about the gallery minstrels at funerals. We have already mentioned the special funeral hymn composed for Constantine. Perhaps the most famous funeral hymn nationally was "The Dying Christian to his Soul, a celebrated Ode for Three Voices, by Mr Pope", first published about 1770. It is more commonly known as "Pope's Ode", or "Vital Spark", because it begins: "Vital Spark of Heav'nly flame, quit, Oh quit this mortal frame; Trembling, hoping ling'ring, flying, Oh the pain the bliss of dying". It appears in "350 Hymn Tunes" by Gilbert H.W.Harrison, 1888, and was copied into innumerable manuscript books, including Thomas Prisk's large book already mentioned ("The Dying Christian. A Celebration Ode by Pope, set by Harwood"). The West Gallery Music Association performed it at their music weekend in Ironbridge in 1990, and (playing on the ophicleide) I thought it was a most moving experience. However, there was probably rather less musical talent at most village funerals.

Other funeral hymns were more specifically morbid. John Probert quotes the first verse of a Methodist hymn very popular in Cornwall:

> *"Ah, lovely appearance of death!*
> *What sight upon earth is so fair?*
> *Not all the gay pageants that breathe,*
> *Can with a dead body compare.*
> *With solemn delight I survey*
> *The corpse, when the spirit is fled,*
> *In love with the beautiful clay*
> *And longing to lie in its stead."*

Funerals were very well attended in the old days. 500 people attended William O'Bryan's mother's funeral at Bodmin in 1821, and 1000 miners walked in procession at Captain Josiah Thomas' funeral in 1901. John Probert also tells us that even in the 1930's there were singing funerals at Four Lanes, and at Stithians walking funerals continued during the second World War. Walking funerals continue to this day, for example at Nanpean and Roche.

The West Briton newspaper for 21st April 1837 described burials in Breage: "In other parts of the country.... the friends and neighbours only of a deceased person attend the funeral; and they generally returned without going to a public house, but in this populous district it was not so, the friends usually go from the grave to the public house, and if a funeral is on a Sunday it is made a kind of holiday walk for all the young people within several miles who hear of it. On their coming to the churchtown, the public houses are at once crammed to excess, and a shameful scene soon ensues".

The same newspaper for 29th April 1853: "On Tuesday great excitement prevailed in Marazion, in consequence of the Rev. N.S.Collins, the present officiating curate, refusing to admit the corpse of the late William Williams, sen., into the church, and to perform the funeral rites according to the custom of the place, because the friends of the deceased would not pledge themselves that there should be no singing in connection with the funeral procession through the streets from the church to the burial ground, a distance of some three or four hundred yards – a custom which has been generally observed from the time of the first interment in this place. After keeping the widow and other relations and friends of deceased at the church door till a large concourse of people was collected, whose feelings were excited to a high pitch of indignation, and after much entreaty and remonstrance, the clergyman at last consented

Churchyard of St Mary's, Pydar Street, Truro, where Mr Harvey was buried in 1858.

to the corpse being taken into the church. After the lessons were read, it was taken to the place of interment with singing, and again at the gate of the burial ground the friends were kept waiting for the minister until their patience was nearly exhausted, but at length the rev. gentleman arrived and performed the remainder of the service at the graveside, after which an anthem was sung near the spot, but outside the churchyard enclosure".

When there was a funeral at Trewithian they used to walk over a mile to St. Gerrans singing funeral hymns. The bearers took it in turns to carry the coffin.

However, highest marks must go to the Truro Buildings Group, for publishing in 1988 "From Moresk Road to Malpas", including an account of the funeral of Mr Harvey in 1858. He was the landlord of "The Miner's Inn" in Factory Lane, Truro, and was very popular. No wonder, because he opened his pub on a Sunday outside legal hours.

"When he died in 1858, his funeral was attended by a large number of his friends from the Chacewater district and the proceedings which took place were colourfully reported in the local press. The newspaper heading was "Scandalous Disturbances".

"On Thursday afternoon last, a parishioner of St. Clement was due to be buried in St. Mary's churchyard. The deceased had kept the Miners Inn and it was represented to the clergyman that many from the neighbourhood of Chacewater desired to attend – to whom the usual time for funerals of four o'clock would be inconvenient – he postponed it...to 5.15pm. It appeared that the plan was only a pretence to obtain time for a most offensive and prolonged display of their fancied musical abilities. They brought with them a wretched brass band with which they paraded the streets before the corpse for more than an hour and a half, shouting hymns to its accompaniment. At 4.15 pm they passed St. Mary's church when the funeral bell tolled as usual. The Rev. Harvey went to the churchyard early so as not to keep them waiting but it was not until 5.50 pm having paraded round the town that the procession arrived back at the churchyard – for yet another hymn! As it was almost time for the regular evening service they were pressed to begin the funeral service at once but, having finished the first hymn, they struck up yet another. By this time it was too late and the scheduled evening service began. The crowd took the coffin into the chapel where their conduct during evensong was disgraceful, and they talked aloud, complaining of the length of the service. Immediately after evensong they struck up "Vital Spark" by the side of the grave and, although they were told by the clergyman that it could not be permitted, he was powerless to prevent them and his demand of the names of the ring-leaders was met with scoffs and insults. He was hustled and threatened and they determined to waylay him in the road and tear the parson to bits. Fortunately a back door opened from the churchyard into a back lane and by that means he escaped".

CHAPTER SIX

EPILOGUE

G enerally speaking the harmonium, organ, or barrel-organ meant the end for the old church gallery minstrels. When Falmouth Bible Christian chapel bought a new harmonium in 1876, the local newspaper commented that Nebuchadnezzar's band had gone. It might be thought that organists were immune to the shortcomings of the minstrels, but this was not always so. John Probert tells of one in the Redruth area who got the sack, and departed in a blaze of glory by playing "Goodbye, don't sigh, wipe the tear baby dear from your eye". Before the war an absent-minded chapel organist played for a voluntary "Put me amongst the girls".

Surprisingly, some churches and chapels kept an instrument or two to play with the organ.

Lewannick church had an organ in 1832, because in that year they paid Mr Prouch to repair it. We do not know exactly when they bought it. But in 1835 they bought strings and a bow for their violoncello, in 1837 they bought a bag for it, and they bought strings for it in 1836, 1837, 1838, 1839, and 1840. They seem to have had a cello at least eight years after they installed their organ, and kept the cello in playing order all that time.

At Port Isaac Methodist church they had a harmonium, and for some years Mr Parsons played the violin alongside it. They bought a pipe organ in 1920.

Sticker chapel bought a harmonium and a flute at the same time in 1856.

Kenwyn bought a cello in 1845, after they had bought a barrel-organ in 1824.

The choir at the Teetotal chapel, St. Ives, were accompanied by an organ and a cornet in 1896.

Paynter's Lane End chapel had a bass viol and flute with the organ, Saltash Wesleyan chapel had a bass viol and clarinet with an American organ, and St Ives Methodist New Connexion chapel had a French horn and clarinet with the organ in 1898. Helston Wesleyan chapel had a trumpet to accompany their organ each Sunday from about 1910-1920, and Camelford Victoria Road chapel had a violin and harmonium until 1959.

Redruth Highway Primitive Methodist chapel had a piccolo with the organ in about 1920. The piccolo player had two different instruments, one for the sharp keys, and one for the flat keys. Once after starting a hymn he said "Wait a minute while I change them over", and the organist had to start again. He would play his own descant to a hymn, and the dribble from the piccolo dripped onto the organist's shoulder. (The last two paragraphs are by courtesy of John Probert).

These isolated instances do not really prove that the gallery minstrels were still going strong – after all, the organ is often supplemented by a few instruments today for special occasions. At North Tamerton in 1884 the demise of the gallery minstrels was actually celebrated with a cello and two flutes accompanying the harmonium.

"The North Tamerton Church Choir sang in Surplices in the chancel of the church for the first time on Easter Sunday, April 13th, 1884". 17 choir members were listed, led by Major Holt. "The harmonium (lent to the church by Major Holt) was played by Miss Marion L. Smith; violoncello by Wm John Webber, and the two flutes by Messrs Wm Sargent and Thomas Gay".

Then in 1887 the parochial council agreed: "That the said John Webber be appointed to play the Harmonium in the church under the following conditions: Salary £10 per year, to be paid quarterly; duties commence Lady Day 1887. Duties consist of playing the harmonium at morning and afternoon services every Sunday and on other occasions when required, and that he give the choir a practice for at least 20 minutes every Sunday after Afternoon Service, and one Practice every week if required. Selection of Hymns and Music made by Rector and Major Holt. The Rector contributed £7, and Major Holt £3 to ensure the Salary of £10 to Mr John Webber".

It seems as though Major Holt finally got fed up with the minstrels, and made sure they did not re-appear. He even helped the Rector choose the hymns!

It is difficult to put a date on the final death of the gallery minstrels – as indeed it is difficult to date their birth. Nicholas Temperley quotes Task as saying the last band he knew of was at Winterbourne Abbas in Dorset in 1898, but it is pretty certain that Cornwall can beat that. After all, we had 18 bands in 1895 in our churches, not counting our chapels.

We know of two cornets and a trombone at Baldhu Chapel "circa 1900", and we have photographs of Hellesveor Chapel choir in 1911 with cornet, violin, clarinet and tenor horn, and Altarnun Wesleyan choir c.1900 with violin and cello. John Probert tells us of a clarinet in Lowertown chapel until about 1925, 2 violins in South Downs Wesleyan chapel until the 1930s, a cornet in Crelly chapel until 1935, and a violin in Boynton chapel in about 1941. We cannot be sure if they also had organs.

Hellesveor Chapel near St Ives.

This is not counting special occasions, like the small orchestra assembled at St. Pinnock in 1903 for the coronation, or for that matter, myself and my friends playing for Canon Miles Brown at St. Winnow in 1979.

If we search for the last band playing regularly for services without an organ, the record seems to go to Sithney chapel. John Probert says: "In the 1940s there were about 8 instruments, including trombone, cornet, violin and cello. Up to 1976 they had a violin to help lead the singing". He does not say whether or not there was an organ.

I am indebted to a lady from Nancegollan for telling me about her father, Mr Tom Treloar, who "played a clarinet or bassoon, whatever he fancied that day, in Crelly chapel, for between 40 and 50 years, twice a Sunday." This was until 1943, when he moved to Sithney Green, and "joined Sithney Methodist chapel, and played there with 3 or 4 other people. He continued there for about 18 years". He died in 1963 at the age of 86 after a stroke. The lady explained that Mr Treloar played with the harmonium at Sithney chapel Sunday services, but the band alone led the singing for the monthly Band of Hope meetings, which were held in a side chapel without an organ. By a strange coincidence, I once met the gentleman, and bought his (high pitch, simple system) bass clarinet.

We were delighted to hear confirmation of the Sithney band with a letter and photograph from Leslie Jenkin, who was taught the clarinet by Mr Treloar in 1953, and used to play alongside him for morning and evening services. Mr Jenkin says "by the early 1950s the band had more or less disbanded". He recalls that Mr Treloar was very good at playing the bassoon, and he usually played that instrument with the band, although the photograph shows him holding an alto clarinet. I myself saw that instrument and tried to buy it, but unfortunately it had already been sold.

Sithney Chapel band circa 1950, Mr Treloar holding alto clarinet second from right.

From the above, it seems there was a band in a Cornish chapel, playing monthly without the organ, until the 1950s.It looks rather as though the minstrels did not die, they simply faded away.

Serious musicians did not regret the passing of the minstrels. Certainly the chancel choir with its organ accompaniment represented a great improvement from the musical point of view. Apart from anything else, you could see what they were doing! Historians however regret their passing: with all their faults they represented a virile force of village musical talent, and a colourful part of church and chapel life.

The Rev. F.W.Galpin made an interesting point: "By this means, those who had no vocal gifts took their part in the music of God's House, and with their quiet and unsustained accompaniment invited the people to support and swell the strain of praise". Having no vocal gifts myself, I appreciate the sentiment.

In these days of instant tape-recordings, it is easy to forget that the gallery minstrels never had the chance to hear what they sounded like. Furthermore, the congregation could not compare their favourite minstrels with the latest recording of the choir in St. Paul's Cathedral. Perhaps it was just as well.

The sad end of one group of gallery minstrels is explicitly recorded in a local newspaper for 3rd July 1850:

RE-OPENING OF
SHEVIOCK CHURCH

"It is indeed a truly gratifying and encouraging circumstance to observe the happy effect of the choral service in this church. For years the people have been exhorted and entreated to attend Divine worship regularly, to be in their places in proper time, and to join in, and love the social part of the services – but in vain. Empty benches in church and hostile contempt of her ordinances without her pale, seemed the result of ministerial

Organ at Sheviock Church

efforts – for such singing as occasionally filled the aisles, there was little or no preparation – and therefore it produced irreverence rather than zeal. While the Western gallery, with many disorderly occupants, monopolised altogether the privilege of praising the most high, the congregation remained uninterested and unedified auditors. By the harmony of the choral service celebrated in the chancel, we are happy to find that the gallery is comparatively liberated from its former ill-disciplined frequents......... Mr Clarke, the schoolmaster of Sheviock led the choral services on the Seraphine which he played with accuracy and ability".

Sic transit gloria Sundi. *(see footnote)*

(Footnote: This is the author's last fling. He would not let me delete it. "Sic transit gloria Mundi" means "Thus passeth away the glory of the world", so I suppose the above means "Thus passeth a glorious Sunday! Ed.)

Serpent player's grave, Thomas Maynard 1780-1807, Minstead church near Southampton.

SELECT BIBLIOGRAPHY

For a much wider bibliography, the reader is referred to "The Music of the English Parish Church", by Professor Nicholas Temperley, Cambridge University Press, 1979 & 1983.

(The numbers are used in the list of instruments which follows.)

0   Aye,J. Humour Among the Clergy, London: Universal Press, 1931

1   Baines, A. Musical Instruments Through the Ages, London: Penguin, 1961.

2   Baines, A. Woodwind Instruments and their History, London: Faber & Faber, 1943.

3   Baring-Gould, Rev. S. Old Country Life, Methuen, 1892.

4   Barton, R.M. Life in Cornwall (3 volumes) Extracts from the West Briton Newspaper. Truro: Bradford Barton, 1970.

5   Blume,F. Protestant Church Music. New York 1974.

6   Bolitho, P. The Story of Methodism in the Liskeard Circuit 1751-1967, Liskeard 1967.

7   Church of England. Book of Common Prayer, Oxford: Jackson 1768.

7a Cox, D. Madron Parish Church, no date.

8   Davey, M. Hengan, Redruth: Truran 1983.

8a Deacon, B. Liskeard & its People. Redruth: 1989.

9   Dearnley, C. English Church Music 1650-1750. London 1970.

10 Donaldson, A.B. The Bishopric of Truro: the first 25 years, 1877-1902. London 1902.

11 Drake, N. The Harp of Judah - or Songs of Sion. London 1837.

12 Dunstan, R. The Cornish Song Book. London: Reid, 1929.

13 Frere, W.H. Hymns Ancient & Modern, Historical Edition. London: William Clowes, 1909.

14 Galpin, F.W. Notes on the Old Church Bands and Village Choirs of the Last Century, Proceedings of the D.N.M.A.S., 1905, pp172-181.

15 Galpin, F.W. Old English Instruments of Music (1910), 4th Edition, (revised Thurston Dart) London: Methuen, 1965.

16 Galpin, F.W. The Village Church Band: an interesting survival. Musical News V (1893) pp31-2, 56-8.

17 Grove, G. A Dictionary of Music and Musicians, Fifth Edition, London: MacMillan, 1954 (and later editions).

18 Hamilton-Jenkin, A.K. Cornish Homes and Customs, Dent, 1933.

19 Hamilton-Jenkin, A.K. Cornwall and the Cornish. London: Dent, 1933.

20 Hamilton-Jenkin, A.K. The Story of Cornwall. Truro: Bradford Barton, 1962.

21 Hardy, T. Under the Greenwood Tree. London, 1872 (and later editions).

22 Henderson, C. Cornish Church Guide. Truro: Bradford Barton, 1925.

23 Husband, S.T. Old Newquay. Newquay, 1923.

24 Hutchings, A. Church Music in the Nineteenth Century. London, 1967.

25 Jones, R. The Cornubian Tune Book. Penzance: Cornish, 1870.

26 Kempthorne, J.L. Falmouth Parish Church. Falmouth, 1928.

27 Langwill, L.G. & Boston, N. Church and Chamber Barrel-Organs. Edinburgh: Langwill, 1970

28 La Trobe, J.A. The Music of the Church. London: Seeley & Burnside, 1831.

29 Lee, C. Cornish Tales. London: Dent, 1941.

30 Lee, C. Journal. Edited by K.C.Phillipps. Tabb House, 1995.

31 Lee, C. The Portrait of a Cornish Musician, from The City. Letchworth: Dent, N.D.

32 Lee, C. Vale of Lanherne. Redruth: Truran, 1984.

33 Lightwood, J.T. Methodist Music of the Eighteenth Century. London, 1927.

34 Lightwood, J.T. The Music of the Methodist Hymn Book. London: Epworth, 1935.

35 Long, K.R. The Music of the English Church. London, 1972.

36 MacDermott, K.H. The Old Church Gallery Minstrels. London: SPCK, 1948.

37 MacDermott, K.H. Sussex Church Music in the Past. Chichester: Moore & Wingham, 1923.

38 Matthews, J.H. A History of the Parishes of St. Ives, Lelant, Towednack and Zennor in the County of Cornwall. London, 1892.

39 McGrady, R. Music and Musicians in Early 19th Century Cornwall. Exeter: University Press, 1991.

39a Meneage & Lizard Oral History Group. Traditional Life in the Far South West. Lizard, 1980.

40 Middleton, R.A. The Cherry Gardens of Yesterday. Padstow: Lodenek Press, 1982.

41 Miles Brown, H. The Catholic Revival in Cornish Anglicanism, ND

42 Miles Brown, H. The Church in Cornwall. Truro: Oscar Blackford, 1964.

43 Miles Brown, H. Truro Diocesan News Leaflet, Sept 1953.

44 Miles Brown, H. What to Look for in Cornish Churches. Newton Abbot: David & Charles, 1973.

45 Morgan, F. & Button, H.E. The Bristol Tune Book. Bristol, 1881.

46 Osborne, J.A. & Thomas, D.H. Victorian and Edwardian Camborne. Camborne, 1986.

47 Parnall, R. Wreckers and Wrestlers. St. Austell: Warne, 1973.

48 Peter, R. & Peter, O.B. The Histories of Launceston and Dunheved. Plymouth: Brendan, 1885.

49 Pool, P.A.S. A Cornish Farmer's Diary. Hayle, 1977.

49a Probert, John C.C. The Worship & Devotion of Cornish Methodism. Private Publication. 1978.

50 Quiller-Couch, Sir A. The Looe Diehards, from Wandering Heath, 1895.

51 Reynolds, T. The Chapels and Curates of Market Jew (Marazion). Worden.

52 Roberts, J.K. The Mevagissey Independents, 1625-1946. Taunton: Goodman, 1946.

53 Roddis, R.J. Penryn. Truro, 1964.

54 Routley, E. The Musical Wesleys. London 1968.

55 Rowe, D. & Ingrey, J. Padstow and District. Lodenek Press, 1984.

56 Sharp, H.B. Church Band, Dumb Organist, and Organ. Galpin Society Journal XIV (1961) pp37-40.

57 Shaw, T. A History of Cornish Methodism. Truro, 1967.

58 Sternhold, T. & Hopkins, I. The Whole Book of Psalms. London: John Day, 1562.

59 Stithians Local History Group. Stithians III. Stithians, 1984.

60 Sumner, W.L. The Organ. London: MacDonald & Jane's, 1952.

61 Tate, N. and Brady, N. A New Version of the Psalms of David, fitted to the Tunes used in Churches. London, 1696.

62 Telford, J. The Methodist Hymn-Book Illustrated. London: Culley, 1906.

63 Temperley, N. The Music of the English Parish Church. Cambridge: University Press, 1979.

64 Thomas, C. Christian Antiquities of Camborne. Truro, 1967.

65 Truro Buildings Research Group. From Moresk Road to Malpas. Truro, 1988.

66 Truro Buildings Research Group. In and Around St. Clement Churchtown. Truro, 1991.

67 Weir, C. Village and Town Bands. Aylesbury: Shire Publications, 1981.

68 Winstanley, M. High Tide at Port Isaac. Padstow, 1978.

69 Woodhouse, H.G. Cornish Bagpipes – Fact or Fiction? Redruth: Truran, 1994.

70 Woodhouse, H.G. Face the Music! Cornish Studies, One, Second Series. University of Exeter Press, 1993. pp46-61.

71 Woodhouse, H.G. West Galleries in Cornwall. West Gallery, Number 3, Feb 1992, pp25-6

72 Woodhouse, H.G. West Gallery Music in Cornwall. West Gallery, Summer 1993, pp21-7.

72a Woods, Rollo G. Good Singing Still. West Gallery Music Association, 1995.

OTHER SOURCES

73 Carharrack Methodist Museum

74 Church & Chapel Guides (Redruth library, Truro Museum library, and individual churches and chapels).

75 County Record Office, Truro, church accounts, DDP series.

76 .. .. chapel records, MR series.

77 Local Museums.

78 Newspapers – Cornish Times, The Post and Weekly News.

79 Private Communications to the Author.

80 Trewint Methodist Museum.

APPENDIX 1

REFERENCES TO CORNISH INSTRUMENTS

(Numbers in brackets refer to the bibliography). References are to churches unless stated.

ALTARNUN. Clarinet 1848; strings 1856-58; harmonium 1894. West gallery removed 1865. (75).

ALTARNUN METHODIST CHAPEL. Violin, cello, c1900. (80).

ANTONY. Pitchpipe 1785-92; violin 1801-28; bassoon 1801-10; bass viol 1804-28 (replaced in 1822). (75).

BALDHU. Reputed to have had a band. (36).

BALDHU CHAPEL. 2 cornets and trombone c1900. The first cornet player was killed in Wheal Jane in 1910. (79).

BETHEL CHAPEL (St Austell). Strings and flutes. (49a).

BLACKWATER CHAPEL. Bass viol, 1841. (49a).

BOCONNOC. Bass viol 1822-45. (75).

BODMIN WESLEYAN CHAPEL. cello and 2 flutes. (49a).

BOTUS FLEMING. Bass viol 1793-1838. (75).

BOYNTON CHAPEL. Violin until 1941. (49a).

BOYTON. Bass viol 1808-65, clarinet 1808-34, flute 1813, violin 1814-25. (75).

BRADDOCK. Bass viol 1823-47, flute 1808, clarinet 1825. (75).

BREA CHAPEL. 2 or 3 cornets in Sunday school after 1946. (49a)

BREAGE. Mr Dobb made a serpent and seraphine for the church in 1860 (79). Tune book of Mr Trethewey still exists. (79).

BUDE HAVEN (ST. MICHAEL & ALL ANGELS). Built 1835, had gallery, bass viol, flute, violin. Organ installed 1892. (74).

CAMBORNE. Bassoon, bass viol, flute, violin, clarinet c1850. Gallery removed 1862 (64). Barrel organ (36).

CAMBORNE NORTH PARADE CHAPEL. Curtain for orchestra 1866 (49a)

CAMELFORD VICTORIA RD. CHAPEL. Harmonium and violin until 1959 (49a)

CARLEEN CHAPEL. Locally made barrel organ 1834. (57).

CARNON DOWNS CHAPEL. Bassoon and other wind instruments 1837, (74). Cornets, flute, clarinet, euphonium, serpents & bassoons (49a), harmonium 1896, organ 1928. Chapel lit by 80 candles in 1837 (74).

CHARLESTOWN CHAPEL. Bass viol 1841, seraphine 1849 (76).

COLAN. Bass viol 1833-43, clarinet 1835-42. (75).

CONSTANTINE. Ophicleide and flute. Organ 1890. Funeral hymn (74).

CRANTOCK. Bassoon 1790-1847 (new bassoon 1841), clarinet 1817-49 (new clarinet 1827 & 1838), bass viol 1817-54, flute 1817-43 (new flute 1830). (75).

CRANTOCK CHAPEL. String and wind instruments c1910. (49a).

CREED. Clarinet 1785-1808, bassoon 1786-1807, oboe 1789-1808, violin 1805. (75).

CRELLY CHAPEL. Flute & clarinet. Piccolo until 1917. Cornet until 1935. (49A).

CROSSWYN (ST. EWE) CHAPEL. Wind and strings c1815. (52).

DAVIDSTOW. Violin 1850-69, bass viol 1850-69, organ 1877. (75).

DULOE. 2 flutes 1804-06, bass viol 1805-09, harmonium and gallery removed 1860. (75 & 41).

EDGCUMBE METHODIST CHAPEL. (Falmouth circuit). 2 flutes, clarinet, euphonium, serpent, bass viol, ophicleide, late 1800s. Then harmonium, then organ. (74).

EGLOSKERRY. Pitch pipe 1775 and 1791, bass viol 1804-56, violin 1820-55, harmonium 1871. (75).

FALMOUTH BIBLE CHRISTIAN CHAPEL. Band until harmonium 1876 (49a).

FEOCK. Violin 1836-44, bass viol 1836-43, keyed bugle 1836, old bassoon sold 1839 for 5s 0d. (75). It is said that this church had a band of 7 bassoons. (36).

FEOCK, GOONPIPER CHAPEL. Built 1867, gallery removed 1890. Said to have had an orchestra. (74). Bass viol, clarinet, flute 1895 (49a).

FORRABURY (BOSCASTLE). Bass viol 1785-1858, bassoon 1821, 3 flutes 1823, organ 1871. (75 & 74).

GARRAS METHODIST CHAPEL. Clarinet 1850. (73).

GOONOWN CHAPEL. Serpent and bass viol 1853. (49a).

GRACCA CHAPEL (BUGLE). Serpent 1840. (79).

GRAMPOUND RD. WESLEYAN CHAPEL. Violin, cello. (49a).

GREENBOTTOM CHAPEL. Cello. (49a).

GULVAL. Clarinet 1824, barrel organ then finger organ 1847. (74).

HAYLE (ST. ELWIN). Musicians' gallery. (74).

HELLAND. Oboe 1802, bassoon 1806-34, (when it was exchanged for a bass viol), clarinet 1828, bass viol 1834-46. (75).

HELLESVEOR CHAPEL. Cornet, clarinet, ophicleide 1874 (57). Violin, euphonium 1911 (77). Bass viol, piccolo. (49a).

HELSTON WESLEYAN CHAPEL. Bass viol 1862, trumpet with organ c1910-1920. (49a).

HENWOOD CHAPEL. Bass viol. (49a).

ILLOGAN. Bassoon and west gallery 1797-1822, organ 1864. (75).

INDIAN QUEENS EMMANUEL CHAPEL. Violins and flute. (49a).

JACOBSTOWE. Pitch pipe 1774, violin 1827-65, bass viol 1827-65, harmonium 1903, organ 1919. (75).

KENWYN. Pitch pipe 1787 and 1797, reeds 1822, bass viol 1823-25, barrel organ 1824 (but still a cello in 1825). (75). Village orchestra had a bass viol, clarinets, bassoon 1820. There is a picture of "The village orchestra" showing clarinet, serpent, flute, double-bass, violin, bassoon (no date) (74).

KERLEY DOWNS CHAPEL. Bassoon and clarinet until 1930s. (49a).

LADOCK. Cello 1847-62, organ 1888 (75).

LANDULPH. Bass viol 1825-48, violin 1825-47, harmonium 1859. (75).

LANEAST. Possible serpent 1799 (writing unclear) (75).

LANIVET. Clarinet, bass viol early 19th century, organ 1871. (79).

LANLIVERY. Flute 1857, cello 1863, harmonium 1871. (75).

LANNER WESLEYAN CHAPEL. "Instruments" 1844, serpent 1857, flute, serpent and "horselegs" pre 1889. (49a).

LANREATH. Pitch pipe 1796 and 1812, bass viol 1806-47, violin 1808-47, clarinet 1825-31, flute 1825, gallery 1834. (75).

LANTEGLOS-BY-FOWEY. Bass viol 1848-58, harmonium 1884. (75).

LAUNCESTON METHODIST CHAPEL. "Instrumentalists" 1829, (57). Bass viol 1815. (49a).

LAWHITTON Bass viol 1812-21, organ 1888. (75).

LELANT. "Band" 1737, gallery 1751, pitch pipe 1760, organ 1908. (75).

LESNEWTH. Pitch pipe 1812-16, harmonium 1877. (75).

LEWANNICK. Pitch pipe 1776-89, bass viol 1807-40, violin 1811, organ 1832 (with bass viol), harmonium 1872. (75).

LEZANT. "Minstrels, choir, and singing-loft". (74).

LINKINHORNE. Bass viol 1801-28, violin 1817-23. (75).

LISKEARD (ST. MARTINS). Gallery 1824-32, violin 1826-28, bass viol 1826-28, organ 1844. (75). "Violins, cellos, flutes, clarinets, bassoons and scorpions, to make sweet music for the good people of Liskeard". (74).

LISKEARD (GREENBANK CHAPEL). 2 cornets, 3 flutes, 2 or 3 violins, double-bass. (6), (49a).

LISKEARD (NEW WESLEYAN CHAPEL). 2 violins, 2 or 3 flutes, cello, double-bass 1841.

LITTLE PETHERICK. Bass viol 1818-58, 2 flutes 1858. (75 & 74).

LOOE (EAST). Flute 1811, harmonium 1873. (75 & 74).

LOWERTOWN CHAPEL. Clarinet until c 1925. (49a).

LUDGVAN. Gallery 1798-1833, bass viol 1824-56, violin 1837-56, clarinet 1839-53, bass horn 1856, organ 1860. (75 & 74).

LUXULYAN. Gallery 1806, pitch pipe 1806, clarinet 1815-43, bassoon 1816, bass viol 1822-23, flute 1832, harmonium 1870. (75).

MABE CHAPEL (TRENOWETH). Ophicleide, 2 fifes c1880, Serpent 1846. (79).

MADRON. "Orchestra" 1750 (7a). bass viol 1806-38, 2 clarinets 1808-27, violins 1813-14, gallery 1836, flute 1827, "organ" 1840, barrel organ until 1859. (75 & 74).

MAKER. Before 1874 had gallery, flute, pitch pipe, then harmonium, then organ 1875. (74).

MARAZION (MARKET JEW). Bass viol 1805-14, gallery 1841. (51 & 75).

MAWNAN. Gallery 1803-25, "bass reeds" 1828, clarinet 1832, organ 1906. (75).

MENHENIOT. Pitch pipe 1793, organ 1804. (75).

MEVAGISSEY. Flute 1845, strings no date, harmonium 1855. Poem describes clarinet, flute, oboe, cello, violins. (52).

MORWENSTOW. Bass viol 1813-63, violin 1813-63, gallery 1848, harmonium, organ. (75 & 74).

MOUNT HORAM CHAPEL. Cello. (49a).

MOUSEHOLE. Violin, bass viol, flute c1860. (57).

MOUSEHOLE WESLEYAN CHAPEL. Violin, viola, bass & French horn until harmonium 1879. Organ 1903. (49a).

MULLION. Fiddles, bass viol, bassoon, cornet, no date, (38a).

NEWLYN EAST. Gallery 1823, clarinet 1835, strings 1835, harmonium 1868. (23).

NEWQUAY (CHURCH OF ST. MICHAEL). Flute 1858, organ 1881. (23).

NEWQUAY (WESLEYAN CHAPEL). Cello 1852. (23).

NORTH HILL. Strings 1829-40, gallery 1847, organ 1908. (75).

NORTH PETHERWIN. Gallery 1813, bass viol 1851. (75).

NORTH TAMERTON. Pitch pipes 1783, bass viol 1794-1884, flutes 1884, harmonium 1887, organ 1891. (75).

OTTERHAM (CAMELFORD). Gallery 1823, strings 1823. (75).

PADSTOW. Gallery 1817, bass viol 1818-52, flute 1834. (75).

PENMARTH CHAPEL. Tenor horn, cornet, flute, bassoon, double-bass in former times, 2 cornets, euphonium, clarinet & flute until c 1912. (49a).

PAYNTER'S LANE END CHAPEL. Bass viol & flute with organ (49a).

PENMENNOR CHAPEL (STITHIANS). Brass instruments 1865-78. (79).

PENRYN WESLEYAN CHAPEL. Bass viol, 1 or 2 flutes, serpent prior to organ 1859, harmonium 1888. (53).

PENZANCE "ORGAN CHURCH" WESLEYAN. Band walked out when organ was installed. (79).

PERRANUTHNOE. Bass viol 1818-33, clarinet 1831-34, organ 1884. (75).

PHILLACK. Bass viol 1804-34, clarinet 1809-30, violin 1819. (75).

PORT ISAAC CHAPEL. 3 flutes, bass viol 1848. (49a). Harmonium with violin c1900, organ 1920. (68).

POUGHILL (ST. OLAF'S). Gallery 1779-1860, pitch pipe 1780, flute 1806-19, bass viol 1787-1855, violin 1807-27, harmonium 1875, organ 1882. (75).

POUNDSTOCK (ST. NEOT'S). Gallery 1798-1891, pitch pipe 1783, bassoon 1789, bass viol 1790-1849, violin 1798-1860, oboe 1800-01. (75).

PROBUS. Gallery 1851, "automatic reed organ" c1850. (36).

REDRUTH (ST EUNY'S). Gallery removed 1878, "orchestra" before that, harmonium 1873, barrel organ, organ. (74).

REDRUTH HIGHWAY PRIMITIVE METHODIST CHAPEL. Piccolo & organ c1920. (49a).

RILLA MILL CHAPEL. Serpent, bassoon. (79).

ST. AUSTELL. Gallery 1829, flutes 1831, barrel organ 1820, seraphine 1854, organ 1872. (75 & 74 & 39).

ST. AUSTELL PRIMITIVE METHODIST CHAPEL. Bass viol 1869. (49a).

ST. BLAZEY. Gallery 1826-97, bassoon 1800-06, oboe 1800-04. (75).

ST. BURYAN. Gallery 1851, clarinet 1817, violin 1826, bass viol 1827, harmonium 1880. (75).

ST. CLEER CHAPEL. Cornet 1877. (49a).

ST. CLEMENT. Clarinet 1806, bass viol 1827, violin 1827. (74). "Buzaglio" (79).

ST. DAY WEST END CHAPEL. Brass instrument 1844. (49a).

ST. DOMINIC. Strings 1800-09, bass viol 1808. (75).

ST. ERME. Bassoon 1819. (78).

ST. ERTH. Band played in church in morning and chapel at night. (49a).

ST. ERVAN. Bass viol, now at Little Petherick. (74).

ST. GENNYS. Pitch pipe 1802, violin 1802-55, oboe 1802-07, bass viol 1819-55. (47).

ST. IVES. Gallery 1639-1840, bass viol, clarinet. (38). Barrel organ 1831. (27 & 77).

ST. IVES FORE ST. CHAPEL. Violins, cello, clarinet. (49a).

ST. IVES METHODIST NEW CONNEXION CHAPEL. Organ, French horn & clarinet (?) 1898 (49a).

ST. IVES TEETOTAL CHAPEL. Organ and cornet, 1896. (77).

ST. JUST IN PENWITH. Gallery removed early 19th century.

ST. KEVERNE. Bassoon 1822-24, 2 clarinets 1822. (74).

ST. MARTIN-BY-LOOE. Flutes 1819-47, violins 1819-54, bass viol 1819-54, gallery removed and organ installed 1878. (75 & 74).

ST. MARY'S, ISLES OF SCILLY (OLD CHAPEL). Serpent "played in the chapel, now the cinema hall, in the 1830's" (77).

ST. MARY'S, ISLES OF SCILLY CHURCH. 2 clarinets, 2 violins, bass viol, played in Old Town church, then Hugh Town church until the organ was installed in 1866.

ST. MAWGAN IN PYDAR. 2 flutes, 2 clarinets, 1 or 2 bass viols until gallery removed in 1860, then harmonium. (74).

ST. MELLION. Bass viol 1841-49, organ 1893. (75).

ST. MICHAEL PENKEVIL. Pitch pipe 1778, clarinet 1802-20, bass viol 1838-65, organ 1907. (75).

ST. MINVER. Bass viol 1836, violin 1841. (75).

ST. NEOT. Bass viol 1799-1839, oboe 1799-1803, flute 1804-29, clarinet 1805, violin 1813-23, gallery 1819. (75).

ST. PINNOCK (NEAR LISKEARD). Bass viol 1815-24, "small orchestra" assembled in 1903 for coronation. (74).

ST. PIRAN (PERRANZABULOE). Gallery and string band before 1873. (74).

ST. SAMPSONS. Clarinet 1845, bass viol 1845-60, flute 1853, harmonium 1876. (75).

ST. STEPHENS (SALTASH). Gallery 1788, bass viol 1789-1846, violins 1823-46. (75 & 74).

ST. TUDY. Gallery 1741, pitch pipe 1768 and 1798, "musical instruments" 1809, bass viol 1812-22, clarinet 1817-19, bassoon 1821. (75).

ST. WENN. Oboe 1789, pitch pipe 1809, clarinet 1810-34, bass viol 1820-38, bassoon 1835. (75).

ST. WINNOW. Bassoon 1805-25, 2 flutes 1807-26, bass viol 1813-27, clarinet 1814-26. (75).

SALTASH WESLEYAN CHAPEL. Flutes last century. American organ, clarinets & bass viol. (49a).

SENNEN. Had a band. (36).

SHEVIOCK. Gallery 1741, pitch pipe 1768 and 1790, bass viol 1814-42, 2 violins 1820-42, seraphine 1842 (actually an Aeolophon which is still there). (75).

SITHNEY. "Musical instruments" 1828, bassoon 1836-39, bass viol 1837-38, harmonium 1873. (75).

SITHNEY CHAPEL. Clarinet, bassoon 1943-60. (79). 8 instruments including trombone, cornet, violin & cello in 1940s. (49a).

SOUTH DOWNS WESLEYAN CHAPEL. 2 violins until 1930s. (49a).

SOUTH HILL. Gallery 1777, bass viols 1798-1827, violin 1800-24, organ 1881. (75).

STICKER CHAPEL. Bass viol 1847-56, flute 1856, harmonium 1856. (76).

STITHIANS PENMENNOR CHAPEL. Instruments until organ 1878 (49a)

STRATTON. Oboe 1788-95, violin 1789, bass viol 1795-1845, gallery 1811, organ 1847. (75).

TALLAND. Pitch pipe 1778, bassoon 1790, strings 1809, bass viol 1819-55, flute 1820-38. (75 & 74).

TORPOINT. Bass viol 1808-19, flute 1819, gallery 1819. (75 & 44).

TREGAJORRAN CHAPEL. Serpent, ophicleide, flute c1860. (79). Brass and wind until 1883. (49a).

TREGONEY (ST. CUBY'S). Gallery 1826, flute 1827 (? writing poor), organ 1831. (75 & 74).

TREGREHAN MILLS CHAPEL (ST. AUSTELL). Bass viol 1862. (49a). Flute before harmonium 1880. (74).

TRENEGLOS (BUDE). Bass viol 1805-32, gallery 1805, violins 1831. (75).

TRESMEER. Bass viol 1806-14, oboe 1806-14, violin 1806-14. (75).

TREWEN (LAUNCESTON). Pitch pipe 1797, bass viol 1802. (75).

TRISPEN CHAPEL. Bass viol. American organ 1894. Organ 1929. (49a).

TRURO WESLEYAN CHAPEL. Bass strings 1811. (49a).

TYWARDREATH. Oboe 1785, bassoon 1812, flutes 1815-49, bass viol 1815-27, gallery 1819. (75).

WEEK ST. MARY. Bass viol 1818-62. (75 & 74).

WENDRON (CRELLY CHAPEL). Clarinet, bassoon, other woodwind 1920-43. (79).

WHITSTONE. Violins, bass viol, flute 1864. (78).

ZENNOR. Gallery 1722, bass viol 1830, clarinet 1833. (75). Also flute, violin before 1890. (49).

(numbers in brackets refer to the bibliography)

APPENDIX 2

List of tunes in the tune book (in sequential order) of Hannibal Lugg Lyne of St. Mawgan in Meneage circa 1840. Cornish Methodist Historical Association No 31, County Record Office, Truro, ref X540/63.

Evening Hymn
Belvedere or West
    Cornwall
Ashman
Miles Lane
Devotion
Triphena
Continued and
    Ended
Auburn
LM Petersburgh
Expression
Adelaide
Sheerness
Homerton
Thomas
Pierpoint
Piety
Pleasure
Gabriel
Gladtidings
Ebeneazer New
Zion's Temple
Daniel Street
Hamilton
Mary
Daventre LM
Elizabeth
Benjamin LM
Missionary
Monmouth
Ephesus
Tripposa
Forgiveness
Portuguese Hymn
Cyprus
Liverpool
Old Windsor
Wolsingham
Egloscury
Gibralter
India
Plymouth
Kent
Bethlehem

Pousladden
Devonport
Bridport
The Old Hundredth
St. Austell New
Two Trebles
Acton
New Sabbath
Cambridge
New Court
Abingdon
Ramsgate
Comfort
Doversdale
British
Dunsford
Chasewater
Holy Habitation
Doxology
Euphrates
Doxology (again)
Snertesh Pastures
Innocence
Christ's Hymn (58
    Watts)
Hanover
Evening Hymn
French
Tranquility
Cleft of the Rock
Islington
Bigberry
Evening
Martha
Pisgah's Mount
Trethewey (blank)
Eaton
Hosanna
Axbridge
St. Sarah
Darlington
Endellion
Greetland
Helstone or Burslem
Lidga

Forgiveness
Bath Chapel
Guardian Rock
Malborough or 15th
    Psalm
Grace
Divizes
Hosea
Arabia
Westbury Leigh
South Petherton
Ninwich
Hezekiah
St. Johns
Irish
Christian
St. Austle
Marsh
Samuell
Able
Wrestling Jacob
Saint Clements
Drydens
Tynus
Helston
Segina
Siniock
Mansion
Horsley
Bristol
Glocester
Antigua
Machpela
Israel's Hope
Calynack
Jacob's Ladder
Eglon
Harts
Sithily
Invitatus
Somerset
Lebanon
Savarth (?)
Bradford
New York

Henley
Lonsdale
Francis
Bridgewater (by
    Thomas
    Trethewey)
Castle Cary
Mary Anne
Sarah
Sabbath
Doxology
Thirland
Heber
Persia
Bradly Church
Stoke
Sutton Colefield
Falmouth
Europe
Calvery
Blakemore
Will You Go
Mawgan Chapel
Birdsall
Redemption
Arabia
America
Majesty
Sovereign
Awake ye Nations of
    the Earth
Broads Dismission
The Fall of Babylon
Dismissal

APPENDIX 3

Titles of tunes in the two tune-books (in sequential order) of Thomas Prisk of Illogan c1838, in the archive of the Cornish Music Guild.

Triumph
Munich
Liverpool
Charlton
Donington
Exertion
Perell
Zions
? by S.Davey, Crowan
Walsiugham
Francis
Monmoth LM
   Transport
Tyrus
Salestury
Jerusalem
Salem
Tuckers
Lydia (Ledga)
Ephesus
Nehemiah
Kent
Coke
Coke (again)
Ebenezer
Devizes
Gabrel
St.Austll
Tuckers
Kentons
Dover
Bolton Thomas
Piety
Lansdown
Bridport
39 CM
Hesiehiah
Samuel
Darlington
Lunix
Majesty
Jublee
Reading, Redruth
   Church
Bridgewater
New York
Bradley church

Pidkam (?)
Aron 4 lines 7 Arnold
New Easter
Lagina
Fonthill Abby
Transport
Forgiveness
Martha
Mount Hermon
Mariners
Ceylon
Otley
Manshans
Hosea
Womack
Love
Samuel
Manchester
Thomas
Hosea
Doxology
Help
Kingswood
Pope's Ode, set by
   Harwood
Aribia
Rebuen
Glory of Padary
Drydens
Sanctuary by
   J.Purday
Songs of Lion
Judgment
Kimboton
Issril Hope / Israel's
   Hope
Burnham
Manchester
Cleft of the Rock
Pikims
Johnson
Ascension
Johnson
David
Harvest Home
Linards

Sing All in Heaven by
   William Eade
Thomas Prisk. Josia
King Street
Bethlehem
Ebenezer
Jeremiah
Chertsey
Judgment
Funeral Anthem
Nativity
Rejoice
Chapel (?)
Piesmerth
Crostick
Sprospect
Auburn
Bath Chapel
Northampton
Arabia (Aralia)
Plymouth
Lingham
Gidgen
Adoration
Peculiar Meter
Caroline
Sarah
Bristol
Cranbrook
Knaresbiragh
St. Austle by
   D.Tagg(?)
New Irish
Irish
Active
Shirland
Sutton Colefield
Sarah
Stoak
Falmouth
Persia
Ceylon
Town Hlue (?)
Stanns
Friendship
Arnolds
Innocence

Mary

Harmony
Trethewey
Paradise
Pierrpont
Missionary
Hanover
Diadem
Trenorgie by
   B.T.Nennose
Tribunal
Psalm 13
Trenety
Salam
Triumphant Advent
Helston
Little Pilgrim
Ewell
Behold a Virgin
Crucifixion
Christmas Hymn by
   Joseph Pryor
Job
Mohemilla (?) by
   Campbells
Heavenly Music by
   Joseph Pryor Live
**(END OF LARGE
TUNE BOOK)**
Calcutta
Calvary
4 Chant
16 Chant
Help
Manshans
Salutron to our God
Tabernacle by
   A.Dunstan
Carn Brea
Mount Ephraim
Simplicity
Finsbery
Sarah
Suton Colefield
Fonthill Abby
Falmouth
Bradley Church

Cranbrook
Fins Hill by
    A.Dunstan
Suton Colfield
Francis
Dover
Martins
St. Jude's
Galilee
Bond Street by
    A.Dunstan
East Gate
St. Leven
Inocene
Aribia
Harmonia
Kent
Bridport
Ebenezer New
Trenety
Prouston Lodge
Adoration
Missionary
Ephesus
Coke
Ebenezer
Safe Departure
Hanover
Hope by A.Dunstan,
    Redruth
Jerusalem
Piety
Gabrel

Arnolls
Wentworth by
    Abraham
Dunstan, Redruth
The Water of Life
The Ten
    Commandments
The Children's
    Jubillee
Soul's Day
Duet Moderato
Nearer Home
for Jesus
Devizes
Our Victory
Wont You Volunteer
The Morning Star
Stella
Old 100
Redruth
Wareham
Monmouth
Salutation
Phisgah Mount
Doversdale
Donongton
Adoration
Kentons
Tyrus
Green Lane by
    A.Dunstan,
    Redruth
Drydens

Leave Pool
Dunstans by
    A.Dunstan
Resignation by
    A.Dunstan
Chelea
Tribunal
Ceglar (?)
Tamer Terrace
Pereu
Job
Providence
Palestine by
    A.Dunstan
Portreath
Mariners
New Hark
Worweck
Reward
Poland
O How Amiblle
Port Land
Iridriver
Red River
Greenwich New
Bosworth
Adoration
Redemption
Eglin
Josaih
Evening Hymn
Capernaum by
    A.Dunstan

Pilgremage by
    A.Dunstan
Kehelland by
    A.Dunstan
Devotion
Mount Calvary
Affection
Northampton or
    Parkers
Mercy
Evening Song by
    A.Dunstan
Boscroggon Chapel
    by A.Dunstan
Manshans
Gays
Helston
Sagina
Forgivness
Sandhill
Arabia
Lunix
Delight
Knowlton
Harmony
Stanns
Paradise
Praise
**(END OF SMALL
TUNE BOOK)**

APPENDIX 4

Titles of tunes in the tune-book (in sequential order) of Miss Harris,
Tregorrick Methodist chapel, c1890.

Piety
Gideon
Monmouth
Our Better Home
    Beyond
St. Austell
St. Agnes
Praise
Eglon
Old Trumpet Metre
Holingsworth
Malta
Josiah
Arabia
Ephesus

Kenton
Innocence
Aaron
Trinity
Mariners
Stourbridge
Adoration
Israel's Hope
Bradley Church
Pisgah's Mount
Lydia
Salvanus
Martin
Silchester
Hanover

Haverhill
St. Bernards
Chelsea
Mount Ephraim
Hursly
Welsh's
French
Arnolds
Wareham
Churchward
Luthers
Melcombe
Huddersfield
Belmont
Unity

Luthers Chant
Ernan
Sarah
Sprowston
Swafield 8 Psalm
Colnstock
Plymouth
Lillie
Retreat
St. Clare
Blockly
Elim
Bless the Lord, O my
    Soul

INDEX

(Tune titles are not included, neither are the contents of Appendix 1.)